SNAP-SHOT

A friendly greeting awaiting visitors at Kinshasha Airport reads: 'Welcome to Zaire. Enjoy your stay. No photographs at the airport. Anybody taking photographs will be SHOT DEAD.'

Also by Graham Nown

CRIMINAL RECORDS
BYE BYE BIRDIE

A WING AND A PRAYER

Plane Tales from the Arrival Gate

Graham Nown

Futura

A Futura Book

Copyright © Graham Nown 1989

First published in Great Britain in 1989
by Futura Publications
A Division of
Macdonald & Co (Publishers) Ltd
London & Sydney

ISBN 0 7088 4210 0

Photoset in North Wales by
Derek Doyle & Associates, Mold, Clwyd.
Reproduced, printed and bound in Great Britain by
Hazell Watson & Viney Limited
Member of BPCC plc
Aylesbury, Bucks, England

Futura Publications
A Division of
Macdonald & Co (Publishers) Ltd
66–73 Shoe Lane
London EC4P 4AB
Member of Maxwell Pergamon Publishing Corporation plc

ACKNOWLEDGEMENTS

The stories in A WING AND A PRAYER were collected from friends, interviews and newspaper stories. Special thanks go to William Amos, Alistair Carnell, Paul Hick, Andrew Rosthorn, Andy Stevenson, Kevin Rowley, *Executive Travel*, *Business Traveller*, *Flying*, *Stress Today*, the *Daily Telegraph*, the *Sun* and the Oddfax Collection.

CONTENTS

FLIGHTS OF FANCY

It's fear, of course. Even the most seasoned traveller admits to being a little unsettled about flying. Not so much the unreasonable worry of plummeting like a stone from 35,000 ft, but because the whole business of getting from A to B in a most unnatural manner triggers off deep inhibitions.

Airports have never been user-friendly – vast echoing halls which give no clue to which country you might be in. Small wonder that one man, as we shall see, wandered off a plane in New York and believed he was in Rome. With one or two exceptions airports have all the warmth and charm of the Warsaw underground. Gloom pulsates from every row of weary travellers, lying dejectedly across seats, or clutching bundles of personal possessions like the inhabitants of Coronation Street on the night they were evacuated to the mission because of a gas leak.

Pilots, of course, distance themselves from it all, striding purposefully through the great unwashed with door-to-door salesmen's bags, safe in the knowledge that no-one dare speak to them. In thousands of miles of travelling I have never seen anyone ask a pilot for a light, the time of day or change for a fiver. It would be rather like asking an obstetrician for a nappy pin, or offering the Ayatollah Khomeini a pint of Old Peculiar.

This ice-cool insularity works perfectly to keep the punters at arm's length, but hardly helps pilots to win friends and influence people. As a result, whenever they crack a joke over the intercom, it always falls embarrassingly flat. And if they stray from the standard in-flight information they usually reveal some unsettling eccentricity.

I once awoke from fitful sleep on a long-haul return from the Far East to hear the pilot announcing that we were flying over the birthplace of Adolf Hiter. Not only did I, and 300 other people, not particularly wish to know that, but it was the dead of night and we were 37,000 ft up. The news was received with a stunned silence.

This little volume is proof that all who fly for a living are indeed human. Some, like the pilot who grounded his plane because his sausage and bacon breakfast was not served on time, add a certain spice to flying. The knowledge that you are in the safe hands of magnificent eccentrics makes *Airplane* seem like a Tupperware Party.

Perhaps, like one shocked businessman, you may find yourself forced into a lavatory by an oversexed stewardess. But, as that kind of thing usually happens to someone else, it is more likely that, like another passenger, the loo handle will simply come off in your hand, leaving you trapped for the duration of your flight.

Either way, it certainly takes the tedium out of travelling.

UP, UP AND AWAY

The excitement of flying usually begins on the ground. Step onto a moving walkway, and who knows where it may take you.

In the case of a Fleet Street travelling companion it was into the arms of the law as an illegal immigrant. His first mistake was to accidentally pick up the suitcase of an attractive Australian girl, identical to his own, at Singapore Airport.

His second was when he found that his section of the moving pavement took a sudden right onto a branch line which led straight out of the airport.

When security men picked him up, hammering on a glass door to get back in, they went through his luggage. In addition to having no travel documents he had to explain that he had never seen the silk underwear and suspender belt in his life before. Never has one journalist come so close to starring in his own exposé.

This, however, is tame stuff compared with the traveller kidnapped by a strange family ... the billygoat made impotent by low-flying aircraft ... and the passengers forced to run a race to claim their seats ...

TICKETS PLEASE

The *Daily Telegraph* reported an exchange in 1986 between an elderly couple about to embark on their first flight, and a Manchester Airport information girl.

On asking why their flight had been delayed, the old lady was told, 'There is a crew change, madam.'

'There you are, dear,' she told her husband triumphantly, 'We do change at Crewe.'

THE MISSING SOAP SYNDROME

When a Pan-Am accountant gets his teeth into a problem, it seems that nothing will deter him. A stock-check of the gin and whisky miniatures served in-flight revealed that they were disappearing at a rate beyond the consumption of even the most inebriated traveller.

Someone had the bright idea of fixing a timing device to the spirits locker to log when the door was opened and sealed. If the door was opened outside flying hours, the thinking went, then the ground crew might be responsible.

It was a pity no-one thought to tell the cabin staff what was going on. An eagle-eyed stewardess spotted the ticking device clamped to the locker and concluded that someone had planted a bomb on the aircraft.

The 747 diverted across Europe and made an unscheduled landing at Berlin, where passengers were evacuated down emergency shutes. The entire panic, Pan-Am estimated, cost the company $15,000. The miniatures were worth thirty-five cents each.

Such enthusiastic sleuthing was rivalled only by a predicament of Basil Fawlty proportions encountered by passengers waiting to take off from Gatwick for Gambia, West Africa, in 1984.

The pilot ordered everyone off the aircraft because two ashtrays were missing, presumably liberated by souvenir hunters on the previous flight. Passengers trudged back to the terminal while ground staff scoured the airport for two replacements.

When they could not find any, the A310 was officially grounded by British Caledonian until new ashtrays were flown in from a warehouse in France by the German airline Lufthansa.

The passengers, tried beyond endurance, had to retrieve their baggage and transfer to another aircraft for the long haul to Africa.

The Civil Aviation Authority later explained that the captain was worried that the two passengers without ashtrays might have stubbed their cigarettes out on the carpet.

A SIGN OF THINGS TO COME?

The world's first scheduled airmail service had a VIP send-off in 1918, with the President of the USA himself waving off the aircraft from Washington. On the flight to Philadelphia, the pilot lost his way and ended up in Waldorf, Maryland. The mail was delivered to Philadelphia by rail.

Some years later, the fickle finger of fate settled on pilot Douglas Corrigan as he climbed into the cockpit to fly from New York to Los Angeles. After a minor misreading of the compass he touched down the next day in Ireland. The greatest navigational gaffe in flying history earned him the nickname 'Wrong-Way

Corrigan' – and a tickertape welcome when he arrived back in New York to try again.

THE DAY THEY WELCOMED WHATSHISNAME

Heathrow has seen some emotional family reunions, but perhaps none so memorable as the day the Williams family assembled at the arrival gate in 1975.

Surrounded by her sisters, Mrs Josephine Williams waited anxiously for the first glimpse of the brother she had not seen for many years.

An unsuspecting traveller, hurrying out with his briefcase, was surprised to find himself being hugged and back-slapped by a group of strange women, and almost bodily carried to the terminal car-park. With some desperation he tried to escape as they bundled him into a waiting car and, at one point, attempted to fling himself from the passenger door as it sped away.

When the excited sisters told him he was being taken to Coventry, the man – on his first visit to Britain – offered them his wallet in exchange for his freedom. He eventually made his bid during a stop en route, and was found cowering behind a farm vehicle.

Mrs Williams said later, 'I thought from the beginning he wasn't my brother, but my sisters wouldn't listen. They said I was only twelve when he left for America, and wouldn't remember.'

THE LATE, LATE SHOW

It isn't that Pan-Am are often late, but an issue of their in-flight magazine *Clipper* felt the need to reassure passengers that 'with few exceptions tickets are always available at London theatre box offices on the day of performance, or soon thereafter.'

ARTHUR'S ANGELS

Manchester Airport has a policy of allowing only urgent Tannoy messages to be broadcast for passengers. The administration office was bombarded with complaints when an appeal went out for 'the person meeting three unaccompanied minors.'

Why, demanded vociferous protestors, should the rules be broken for the likes of National Coal Board pit workers?

AIRBORNE INCONVENIENCE

Chris Elkins, of Addlestone, Surrey, was taking a shower in his bathroom in 1971 when he was distracted by a loud thump from the garden.

Mr Elkins and his wife were rather astonished to find a huge block of ice, half buried in their lawn. It was only when puzzled local policemen removed it for storage in the station refrigerator that someone identified it as frozen urine.

'What with the number of aircraft about,' a police spokesman said, 'we were very lucky it wasn't something worse.'

THREE COINS IN THE HUDSON

If airports are designed for the safe passage of even the most inept traveller, someone must have overlooked Nicholas Scotti, of San Francisco.

Scotti's odyssey began in 1977, when he left the West Coast to visit his family in Italy. At New York's Kennedy Airport the aircraft touched down to refuel and take aboard new passengers.

Thinking he had landed in Rome, Signor Scotti disembarked and searched for the two nephews who were supposed to be meeting him at the arrival gate.

Baffled by their absence, he spent two days scouring the Big Apple for his lost relatives. Nothing could shake Signor Scotti's conviction that he was in Italy. Even when he stopped a policeman to ask directions, the officer answered in fluent Italian.

After riding round the city on a bus for twelve hours, looking for his family, the driver handed him over to the police who tried to prove to Signor Scotti that he was in the USA. As they drove him, protesting, back to Kennedy Airport to catch a flight back to San Francisco, he remained unconvinced.

'I *know* I'm in Italy,' he insisted, pointing out of the patrol car window. 'Look – that's how they drive.'

This was perhaps only marginally more mind-boggling than the saga of German tourist Edward Kreuz, who wandered off an aircraft while it was refuelling in Bangor, Maine. It was only after four days tramping the town searching for the Golden Gate Bridge that he realized he was not in San Francisco.

16

THE GREAT CIRCLE ROUTE

Two French sisters – Simone Yvonne, sixty-nine, and Roben Mariotto, seventy-eight – flew, with little grasp of English, to see a relative in Portland, Oregon.

The first leg of the journey, from Paris to London, was accomplished successfully. From there they flew to Seattle, where all that remained was a thirty-minute local hop by shuttle to Portland.

Unfortunately the last lap took longer than they thought. Two hours into the flight they plucked up courage to ask if they were on the right aircraft.

'I'm afraid this flight is going to London,' the stewardess told them.

Many hours later, back at Heathrow, the two old ladies tried again.

SOME GUYS HAVE ALL THE LUCK

Flying fan Chris English has travelled almost half a million miles on fifty-six different airlines – and only lost his baggage twice.

NO KIDDING

Flying, as some of us know, can have the most profound effect on physical and mental well-being. Among those whose performance became markedly jaded was Drusus, the stud billygoat.

Drusus was renowned throughout Lockerbie, on the Scottish Borders, for his sexual prowess until the RAF began to use the valley for low-level practice runs. He became so agitated at the sight of an RAF fighter that the local vet had to administer injections to calm him down. Then, to make things worse, Drusus lost all interest in the opposite sex.

The story had a happy ending. The Ministry of Defence paid on undisclosed sum to compensate for Drusus's distress and the jets abruptly took Lockerbie off their regular flight path.

At the last report, Drusus, according to his owner, Mrs Mo butcher, was back in 'peak form'.

THE CAR LEAVING FROM RUNWAY ONE ...

Airports may be designed to enable passengers to find their way around easily, but the maze of roads surrounding them can be a minefield for the unwary.

One driver, from Kings Lynn, Norfolk, ended a trip to Luton Airport in hospital when he took a wrong turn into a road kept open only for emergency vehicles. With the twists and turns of the airport approach behind him, he would have been forgiven for thinking that he had at last reached the joys of the open road. But the huge empty motorway he was driving down turned out to be the runway.

When all attempts to attract his attention failed, firecrews scrambled in hot pursuit and eventually had to ram him from the tarmac.

DANGER, KIDS AT WORK

Parents guarding a mountain of luggage *and* small children know that in an airport it is extremely unwise to take your eyes off either of them.

At Shannon Airport one small boy's curiosity got the better of him and he pressed a hydraulic button at the foot of the aircraft steps to see what would happen.

The eight-year-old watched fascinated as the hinges of the airliner door buckled, and bent completely out of shape. The jumbo had to be grounded and 320 passengers put up overnight at a luxury hotel while repairs were carried out. Total damage by one small finger: £500,000.

When ingenuity outweighs curiosity, watch out. Two schoolboys, aged thirteen and ten, somehow managed to hitch a free ride by ferry from their Dublin home to Holyhead, and sneaked aboard buses and trains to Heathrow.

At the airport they talked their way aboard an Air India jet for a free flight to New York. At this point on their odyssey, a New York policeman stopped them and put them on a flight back home – free, of course.

The driving force behind the trip: 'We wanted to see Mr T and the A-Team.'

ON YOUR MARKS

One of *Executive Travel* magazine's star alternative awards of 1985 went to the Nigerian airline which found itself overbooked with three times the normal amount of passengers waiting to travel from Port Harcourt to Lagos.

The cock-up had come about because two previous scheduled flights had failed to arrive. Everyone was hotly claiming priority, and confusion reached such a pitch that ground staff telephoned for the army.

The commanding officer knew exactly what to do. Everyone with boarding cards was ordered to the foot of the aircraft steps. On the word 'go' they had to run twice around the plane. The fittest and fastest past the finishing line could claim their seats. True to form, a small group of British businessmen sailed through among the winners.

SNAP-SHOT

A friendly greeting awaiting visitors at Kinshasha Airport reads: 'Welcome to Zaire. Enjoy your stay. No photographs at the airport. Anybody taking photographs will be SHOT DEAD.'

THE QUICK SHUFFLE

The walk-on service on British domestic routes makes flying easier, and a little like travelling by bus – everything moves smoothly as long as you pay for your ticket.

British Airways cabin staff landed in trouble on a Manchester-to-Heathrow shuttle when they completely forgot to collect the fares. By the time they had remembered, the 130 passengers had made a rapid flight of their own.

THAT WILL DO NICELY

When a British Airways flight from Gatwick to New Jersey was diverted to Connecticut, the aircraft had to be refuelled.

For reasons better known to themselves, airport officials refused to allow the airline its usual credit. The pilot and crew had to pool their American Express and Access cards to pay the bill before they could take off again.

A SNIP OF A SNAP

Marketing folk remember it as the Great TWA Camera Caper – the time when the broad sweep of an idea seemed so brilliant that someone forgot the small print.

In 1984 TWA teamed up with Polaroid for an aggressive marketing deal – if you bought a Polaroid camera, price around £16, you were automatically entitled to 25 per cent off any TWA flight, except to London. But nowhere did the offer say the magic words 'only one per customer'.

Before the deal expired thousands realized that they could fly around the USA for £74 or visit, say, Egypt for a mere £240. A St Louis travel agency bought 10,000 Polaroids and advertised cut-price airfares. McDonnel Douglas purchased 1,000 and worked out that it could save £145,000 on employee travel coasts.

Over at Polaroid they were toasting the sales boost in champagne. The company's travel department even bought 2,000 of their own cameras to cash in on cheap flights, too.

A TWA spokesman said at the time, 'Buyers will find a loophole if there's a loophole there, and we left some big ones.'

The history of airflight marketing is pitted with yawning craters many executives would rather forget. A classic example was the American airline which floated a special offer for wives accompanying husbands on business trips.

The company computer effortlessly printed out a list of all men and women who had travelled together in the previous six months, and mailed out details of the cut-price offer. The airline was innundated with letters from angry wives demanding to know more about the women who had accompanied their husbands on business trips.

In an adventurous marketing exercise, prospective customers for a new Cessna Citation business jet were sent live carrier pigeons bearing an invitation to a free trial flight.

'The recipient was asked to release our carrier pigeon with his address tied to its leg,' said a spokesman. 'Some of the recipients ate the pigeons.'

British Airways were among the pioneers of P.R. stress when they sent model Kim Turner to launch their 'We Take Good Care Of You' campaign in Cyprus. Kim, twenty-three, arrived on schedule minus her luggage, which turned up in Zurich.

THE PAIN BARRIER

When Concorde made its first flight over Wakefield, Yorkshire, there was a rash of injuries among spectators gazing skywards and losing their balance. The final count included two broken ankles, three other fractures, numerous sprains and bruises and a motorist injured when he glanced up and ran into the car in front.

WHEN YOU'RE READY, BOYS

'The official opening of the Connacht Regional Airport at Knock has been postponed,' the *Irish Sunday Independent* reported in January 1986. 'It was to have taken place in April but will not now happen until mid-summer. The delay is to allow work to be completed on time.'

JUST THE TICKET

Pub licencee Bill Webster dreamed of opening a restaurant for everyone who groused about in-flight eating – inside a plane.

His opportunity came when Sheik Al Muraibid of Saudi Arabia left his 186-seater Boeing 720 at Luton in 1982 and got a parking ticket for £35,000. The Sheik decided it was not worth paying and abandoned it.

Bill Webster put in a bid for the plane, minus engines and electronics, to put it in the car park of his Manchester pub, the Why Not.

'I might even invite the Sheik for a meal in his own plane,' he said.

OOPS

Council leaders drew up ambitious plans in 1984 to launch Birmingham's £60-million new airport with a Concorde flight. Arrangements had to be scrapped when someone pointed out that the runway was too short for Concorde to land.

In terms of official embarrassment, faces were equally red in 1983 when the Isle of Man's first duty free shop at Ronaldsway was officially opened – and immediately closed. The management had forgotten to apply for an off-licence.

PRIZE TAGS

The elite handful of regular Concorde travellers were rewarded for their loyalty with a gift from British Airways in 1986. The company presented them with commemorative solid silver baggage tags.

A few weeks later a letter followed advising them

not to use them – baggage handlers around the world were ripping them off and pocketing them.

METRIC MIX-UP

Air Canada's evening flight from Montreal to Edmonton in 1983 made its first scheduled stop at Ottawa and took off to resume the 1,000-mile journey.

As passengers were watching a movie high over Winnipeg, the engines went dead. Captain Roger Penn announced that he would have to make an emergency landing, and began a 100-mile glide earthwards.

He landed heavily on a disused airstrip, bringing the aircraft to a halt only yards from a busy sportscar race meeting.

The reason for the accident was that the jumbo, unknown to the crew, had taken off with only half a tank of fuel. Ground staff had confused imperial and metric measures when filling it up.

THE WORLD'S WORST AIRPORT

Some of the approaches to the world's airports are notoriously tortuous and demand a pilot's total concentration. The worst, beyond doubt, is on the island of St Barthélemy in French Guadaloupe, far off the beaten track, but an air traveller's nightmare.

A copy of the local guidebook sums it up: 'It is said that many people would never have heard of St Barth if it were not for its airport. There may be some truth in this if you watch the pallid faces of some of the incoming passengers and there can be no denying, on the part of pilot and passengers alike, the thrill of one's first approach by air.

'Where, you ask yourself, palms moist, can the airport be? Surely not behind that mountain? But it is. Hardly reassuring, a cement cross sweeps past, the aircraft seems to plunge into a bottomless void, and then, miraculously, you are once again on solid ground.

'It's only when you're taxiing back that you notice the cars lined up on a road alongside the runway and the tourists breathlessly poised with their cameras. Without knowing it, you have just been part of an event.'

AIR SICKNESS

A businessman told *Executive Travel* magazine that once he was stranded in Guangzhou, China, and forced to wait seven hours for his plane to take off. With his British patience at breaking-point, he asked an official what was wrong with the aircraft.

'We were finally informed,' he reported, 'that the aircraft was "sick" and that a new one would be found. Two hours later we were told, "New aircraft more sick than first one, so will take first one".'

HOUSE OF DISPLEASURE

Newspapers usually refer to stranded or delayed air travellers being offered temporary accomodation in a 'luxury hotel'. This is generally true, though a vicar en route from Hong Kong to Gatwick in 1982 found the interpretation rather different.

When his British Caledonian DC-10 was unable to take off from Kai Tak because of engine problems, 220 passengers were offered overnight accomodation. The reverend knew that he must have been somewhere near the end of the list when he found himself inadvertently booked into a house of pleasure, with a circular bed and 'room service with extras'.

'The place,' said B-Cal, 'was obviously tailored for people with somewhat exotic tastes, but he was not approached by any lady member of the staff. We have sent him a letter explaining our difficulties and how the problem arose, and hope it will be accepted.'

SWEET B.A.

There was a time when aircrews were fond of inventing their own nicknames for the world's major airlines. Among those which endured longer than most were:

'Bend Over Again Christine' for BOAC

'Queer And Nice Types Of Stewards' for QUANTAS and 'Sweet And Sexy' for SAS.

TWA, for some reason, was known as 'Try Walking Airlines'.

GOLDEN RULES

Among the advice given to passengers by one airline in the 1920s was 'please empty your bladder before embarking.'

Travellers were also wisely warned of the dangers of eating beans, tucking in their scarves in case they tangled with the rudder, and of touching the propeller.

THE MYSTERY OF GRANNY KRASSNOFF

Mitchell Gelfand, fourteen, moved into the Cleveland, Ohio home of his grandmother, seventy-four-year-old Mrs Sarah Krassnoff, in 1970 because she lived near a school he liked. A year later both of them vanished, leaving word that they had gone on holiday.

Mrs Krassnoff, for reasons no-one has ever discovered, took her grandson on one of the longest commuter trips in aviation history. For more than four months they criss-crossed the Atlantic daily, seldom leaving the transit area, and living on in-flight meals. The fares for the 160 crossings cost more than £60,000 which Mrs Krasnoff, a widow, drew from several banks.

The boy's father had started legal proceedings in an effort to find his son, when a neighbour heard on the radio that Mrs Krassnoff had suffered a heart attack in an Amsterdam hotel – within earshot of the jets at Schiphol Airport. After a reunion with Mitchell, Mr Gelfand questioned him for two hours, only to confess, 'I still don't know why they did it.'

HIGH HOPES

In the 1940s, when aircraft began to fly in the stratosphere, high-altitude flying was recommended as a cure for children suffering from whooping cough.

Successful recoveries were also claimed for one case of deafness and another of stuttering.

COUCH POTATOES

In 1964 a jet was flying through the night over the Atlantic when two sleepless old ladies tottered up the aisle in search of the lavatory.

The crew were sitting on the flight-deck studying a vast bank of controls, illuminated in the semi-darkness, when the door behind them opened. One of the elderly ladies blinked around and rapidly withdrew.

'No dear,' the crew heard her say, 'that's not it. There are three men in there watching television.'

SLOW REVENGE

It was getting late and passengers were settling down for the night aboard a 707 heading from New York to London in 1963. Two middle-aged women were deep in conversation, 'chattering away like a couple of magpies', as one passenger put it.

A man sitting behind them tried to sleep, but found it impossible and ordered himself a beer. The chattering went on until, out of sheer exasperation, he rose to his feet and slowly and deliberately emptied the contents of his glass over the wagging heads.

The women stopped abruptly. The matter was not referred to again until breakfast when they both rose

and, without comment, poured two cups of coffee over the man's head.

SUCTION CUP

In the late 1950s aircraft equipment was slightly more Heath Robinson than today's. On one airliner, turbulence dislodged an air cap from a pipe in the lavatory, disrupting the pressurization mechanism. An unsuspecting woman sat on the loo, creating a partial vacuum which made it impossible to get off again. An impromptu repair by the stewardess finally released her.

LEFT HAND DOWN A BIT

The pilot of a Britannia Airways 767 from Tel Aviv made his approach to Manchester in 1985, and discovered that the right-hand wheel had not locked into position.

He circled the control tower while technicians examined the undercarriage through binoculars, and consulted engineers in Israel by radio. After several attempts to lock the wheel, it finally 'looked good'. But the pilot was taking no chances.

He asked all thirty-six passengers to sit on the left-hand side of the aircraft to take the weight off the suspect wheel. When the plane landed safely they broke into a spontaneous round of applause.

OUT OF THE BLUE

One of the greatest aviation mysteries still unresolved centres on two young children who are thought to have survived a fall from a Tri-Star, 29,000 ft above the Persian Gulf.

In 1980 a tyre burst on the landing gear of the Saudi Arabian Airways plane when the wheels were retracted. The explosion blew a two-foot hole in the fusilage through which two young Pakistani children were sucked.

Samina, ten, and her brother Ahmed, six, were never found, despite an extensive search. Three years later there was an amazing twist to the story. A Pakistani, after visiting a small port in Abu Dhabi, claimed to have spoken to a little girl and boy who told him that they had fallen from the sky and were living with an Arab fisherman who rescued them, believing them to be a gift from God.

By the time the Pakistani had alerted the authorities, the fisherman had sailed without mentioning the name of his home port. A painstaking search of small fishing communities along the Gulf failed to find any trace of them.

A slim chance that the children might be alive is not beyond the bounds of possibility. According to Lockheed, when a plane broke up in a storm over the Peruvian jungle in the late 1960s, a little girl fell 15,000 ft, still strapped in her seat, and landed safely in a treetop.

ON YOUR MARKS

The College of Aeronautics at Cranfield advertised for volunteers to take part in three-hour tests to see how quickly an aircraft could be evacuated. The sixty 'passengers' under starter's orders in the Trident airliner were each paid £10. A £5 bonus was offered to the first thirty to fight their way out of the aircraft when the alarm sounded.

SERVICE WITH A SMIRK

The world's first stewardess was a nurse. When Ellen Church climbed aboard for the historic flight from San Francisco to Cheyenne, Wyoming, in 1930, she was ready to deal with any medical emergency. The only drink passengers were likely to be served was a stiff spoonful of stomach medicine.

The world turned many times before Southwest Airlines paid stewardesses a bonus to strip off their uniforms and serve drinks in shorts and skinny sweaters. Rival airlines considered the risk of heart attack among male passengers too high to emulate the service.

Generally stewardesses object to the sexy image airline marketing has given them. I am told, by those who have persevered for years and failed, that there are few chat-up lines which impress them, either. Despite the Sunday newspapers, the sad fact of life, chaps, is that stewardesses have the lowest divorce rate of any women's profession.

The only man ever to succeed instantly was a wealthy rancher who proposed marriage at first sight and was instantly accepted. Along with him, we meet the stewardesses who bite back ... the rare and randy air girl who bundled a passenger into the loo ... and the stalwart stewardess who whipped off her stockings to repair the in-flight movie projector. Ellen Church would have been proud of her.

34

VE HAV VAYS ...

Most passengers disembark quite impressed with the Germanic efficiency of Lufthansa. On occasions, however, staff have been known to let their enthusiasm get the better of them.

One traveller claims to have heard a Lufthansa stewardess conclude her pre-flight drill with, 'You vill now please fasten your seat-belts ... I only vant to hear vun click.'

ONE 747, WITH FRIED RICE

Dazed by bizarre in-flight announcements, or indeed lack of them, readers vied for the most memorable in the columns of the *Daily Telegraph*.

The unrivalled winner of the most staccato reply was that given to the puzzled British passenger on an internal China Airlines flight. When he had the temerity to ask why there was no customary emergency drill, the stewardess shrugged and explained, 'We crash – you die.'

HELLO SAILOR

During safety procedure demonstrations, quite a few travellers are puzzled by that tiny whistle attached to the life jacket.

One stewardess, demonstrating the equipment on a British Airways flight to Jersey explained, in all seriousness, that it was 'to attract the attention of passing sailors'.

At Quantas they are more tongue-in-cheek. Passengers waiting to take off on a flight from Sydney to Norfolk Island were informed, 'And last of all there is the whistle – you can use this to attract the sharks.'

Safety measures are supposed to be carried out to the letter, even when their purpose seems obscure – a point underlined by the stewardess on a Heathrow-to-Manchester trip as she demonstrated a lifejacket.

After the usual explanations of how to cross and tie the tapes, and how the little flashing light activates itself on immersion in sea water, she added, '... which isn't really much use to any of us. We won't be passing over the sea anyway.'

I DO, I DO

In the course of a long flight from New York to Hong Kong Jim Bates, a wealthy Arizona rancher, became heavily smitten by Miss Sue Fan, the attractive stewardess attending him. As the hours passed he felt compelled to tell her that she was the most beautiful woman he had ever seen, and that he had fallen in love with her.

When the plane touched down at Kai Tak he kissed her and asked her to consider seriously marrying him. The girl, taken aback, promised to think it over.

By the following day she had made up her mind and decided to say yes. Unfortunately, she managed to reach the airport only to see his return flight to New York climbing westward. Undeterred, the stewardess found a communications system and radioed the aircraft with her acceptance.

The call was answered by stewardess Dorothy Cooper, who told her, 'Too late, I've just accepted him myself.'

IN-FLIGHT ENTERTAINMENT

An incident which that most superb of airlines, Air New Zealand, would prefer to forget was the suspension of one of its most popular stewardesses.

The reason for her popularity was not unconnected with a memorable flight from Auckland to Honolulu when she ran down the aisle waving her knickers above her head, before forcing a startled male passenger into the lavatory and sexually assaulting him.

It was only when the panic-stricken man was flung against the distress button in an effort to untangle himself that the crew broke down the door and discovered his predicament.

The unnamed passenger on the flight to Hawaii claimed that Stewardess Jane Whitehead, thirty, drank five glasses of champagne and said to him, 'Let's go down the back.'

After the sex session she felt faint and had to be helped into the first class cabin. The aircraft's purser said, 'She fell over, her legs went into the air and it was apparent she was not wearing underpants.' The purser was kneed in the groin when he refused to have sex with her.

The stewardess later told an Auckland arbitration court, 'I don't remember anything.'

WE'LL TAKE GOOD CARE OF YOU

Gatwick Airport's staff magazine *Skyport* carried the bizarre tale of a British Airways stewardess who was married to a bondage enthusiast. She flew to Paris – a six-hour round trip – leaving her happy husband stark naked and trussed like a chicken in the bottom of the wardrobe.

The stewardess planned to release him when she arrived back in London in time for tea. Sadly, the plane broke down and she was told that she would have to stay overnight and fly back the next day. The embarrassed girl, worried about leaving her husband, had to telephone the police and ask them to break into her house and free him.

THE SOUND AND THE FURY

Even on the most sleep-inducing flight, there is always a nagging worry that, unlike driving a car, you can never be quite sure what is going on.

Which perhaps explains why 112 passengers on a Britannia Airways flight from Zurich and Gatwick in 1986 listened open-mouthed as the stewardess calmly announced that the aircraft would shortly be ditching in the sea.

There had been nothing on the flight to indicate an emergency and, to add to the worry, they should not have been flying anywhere near the sea, anyway. While the stunned passengers tried to imagine what had happened, the stewardess explained how to inflate the life jackets, escape from the plane before it sank and swim for the life-rafts.

Several passengers tried to peer through the windows to see how far off course over the ocean they were, but it was difficult to make anything out. The aircraft, meanwhile, hummed happily on, presumably drawing nearer to its doom.

The announcement ended and, as everyone exchanged uncertain glances, there was a long silence. Then the intercom clicked on and the pilot announced that someone had played the wrong tape. What, in fact, they should have been listening to, he explained, was a message about duty free sales.

The incident won *Business Traveller* magazine's Alternative Achievement Award for 1986.

As one 'survivor' later commented, 'We had all been sitting rigid and ashen-faced. You could hear the sighs of relief.'

GAY LOTHARIOS

As all stewardesses know, there are probably no lengths to which the average groper will not go to satisfy his in-flight fantasies.

A popular ploy is to spill his meal deliberately into his own lap and ask a passing stewardess if she would kindly mop it up.

Girls who have been propositioned in this way before have the game-plan worked out in advance with colleagues. They briskly summon a male steward who takes one look at the soiled lap, drops his wrist in delight and coos, 'Are you the gent who requires mopping up, then?'

The stewardess retreats down the aisle, suppressing a smirk, leaving the squirming twerp at the mercy of the enthusiastic steward.

FAIR EXCHANGE

Hard-working cabin staff get a particular satisfaction from bringing pompous passengers down to earth. A British steward with Gulf Air felt his patience wearing thin when an Arab woman in first class pressed the call button every few minutes with various trivial requests.

The flight from London to Bahrain was interrupted in this manner until the baby on her knee had an accident in its nappy. The woman rang for the steward, handed him the child and ordered, 'Change it.'

He walked into the economy class section and asked an Indian woman if she would mind lending her baby for a few minutes. The steward then marched back and placed the strange baby on the troublesome passenger's lap.

'Will this one do?' he asked.

The steward was suspended pending an inquiry.

A far cry from the days of Joan Crane, one of British Airways first stewardesses who flew for years on noisy Dakotas.

'In those days people had beautiful manners,' she said. 'One old lady said to me, "Stewardess, if you have time, would you please clean my shoes?'' I knew I would have time so I said, "Certainly, madam." It would have been very rude of me to refuse.'

SERVICE WITH A SMIRK

The steward on a TWA flight from St Louis to Little Rock summed it up. After he dropped a tray of food in the middle of the aisle, I noticed the badge on his uniform. It read, 'Don't rush me. I'm making mistakes as fast as I can.'

Readers of *Executive Travel* magazine seem also to have experienced the strange wit of cabin staff. One traveller failed to break into helpless chuckles when the steward spilled a can of tomato juice over his white trousers and quipped, 'Oops. But you should see what I do for an encore!'

The Hawaiian sense of humour is equally reassuring. One steward advised passengers, 'Don't be alarmed by the steam pouring in through the ventilation system on this aircraft. It is just peculiar to this type of air-conditioning. If anything were to go seriously wrong, I would be the first to let you know as I left the aircraft.'

The American version is more off the wall. One traveller asked the stewardess how long their flight from Florida to Los Angeles normally took. 'I don't know,' she answered. 'We haven't made it yet.'

Yugoslavians, it seems, take a more relaxed view of life. The magazine reported in 1987: 'Flying JAT to Belgrade after a weekend in Albania (a rigorous travel experience in itself) a reader was asked by the steward for a light for his cigarette, and motioned to get his matches from the bag in the overhead locker.

'The report was given added informality by the fact that the plane was tearing down the runway at the time, with flashing no-smoking and seat belt signs.'

Even when they are doing the job properly, all those in-flight announcements play havoc with passengers trying to snatch some sleep. Especially the alarming message from one stewardess, who informed passengers over the PA system, 'We shall be travelling at 22,000 mph at a height of 620 feet.'

A woman on a flight from San Francisco to London was woken no less than three times by loud duty-free announcements. Bag-eyed from lack of sleep, she stormed down the aisle to complain to the stewardess. 'It gets worse,' she was told. 'Monday we start selling sweaters.'

After such experiences it is heartening to hear that sometimes things do go right. One business traveller was so impressed by the stop-watch precision of a Pan-Am departure to India that he felt moved to call the steward and congratulate the airline.

The steward said that he appreciated the compliment, but it was only fair to point out that it was, in fact, the previous day's flight.

HI-HO, HI-HO

In 1969, Valley Airlines of California ran a fleet of planes so small that they insisted that their stewardesses must be no more than 4ft 10 inches in height. Only one girl in every thirty interviewed passed their stringent standards.

The company's pilots, based in San Jose, measured up to 6ft 2 inches tall.

Just three years earlier, Diana Frith of Canberra was told she would have to wait four months for a job with Trans-Australian Airlines – because her fingernails were too short.

'We do like our girls to be smart and attractive,' said an airline spokesman. 'We think one of the most important points is for them to have attractive-looking finger nails.'

Diana, who had cut her nails because they broke easily, wore false ones. 'I bet lots of air hostesses wear false items to make them look more beautiful,' she said, 'including false eyelashes, false hairpieces and false bras ...'

Interesting points to watch for, Diana.

FINAL APPROACH

A *Daily Telegraph* reader reported the reassuring approach of a Lufthansa stewardess on a commuter service from Frankfurt to Munich. As the aircraft prepared to land for its scheduled stop at Nuremberg, she announced, 'Will those passengers flying to Munich not undo their seatbelts on landing, as our time on Earth is very short ...'

CIRCUITS AND BUMPS

Air Zimbabwe, which advertises itself as 'The Smiling Airline', apparently tries hard to live up to its name. In 1983, eight stewardesses on the state-controlled airline were fired for breach of contract – all had become pregnant.

The sackings were personally ordered by Transport Minister Farai Masango, who said, 'We were able to redeploy stewardesses to other posts. Fourteen stewardesses have benefitted from this policy. But this privilege is now being grossly abused. Many stewardesses seem to thing there is an open season for pregnancies at Air Zimbabwe.'

RING OF CONFIDENCE

It is unusual for passengers to be so pleased with exceptional service that they take the trouble to contact an airline and congratulate them.

This was the case with an alert, attentive, handsome Pan-Am steward who impressed many passengers on his routes. Several of them wrote glowing letters to his bosses, praising him.

Curious Pan-Am administrators decided to look up his employment record, and found that he did not have one. They discovered that the steward, who was still working, was a con-man in uniform. He was arrested and charged with stealing flights worth more than £25,000.

WATER WINGS

One of the more pleasant British domestic flights is the scheduled Air UK service to Jersey, with its spectacular views of the approaching islands.

Passengers may take comfort from the airline's high standards, too. An advertisement for cabin staff placed in local Jersey newspapers required applicants with 'an ability to swim'.

THE SHOW MUST GO ON

The pluck of British Airways stewardesses in an emergency is part of air travel legend. But none deserve more praise for ingenuity than stewardess

45

Linda Starling who was working the New York-to-London route in 1983.

When the projector for the in-flight movie broke down she saved the day by using one of her stockings to replace the broken drive belt.

After fifteen minutes that, too, disintegrated. Stewardess Starling, with selfless presence of mind, used a pair of tights she happened to be carrying to keep the musical *Xanadu* going right to the final frame.

Word of her outstanding devotion to duty reached the ears of John Coleman, UK area manager of Inflight Motion Pictures. He sent a package to Ms Starling with a note: 'Please find enclosed three pairs of replacement take-up belts/stockings. Do not hesitate to contact us if you require help with the fitting.'

While British stewardesses possess a practical streak, their American counterparts have more pizazz. When a projector broke down on a flight from New York to Los Angeles the stewardess found it beyond repair.

A flow of complaints steadily built up from passengers, so she walked through to first class where TV chat show host Johnny Carson happened to be sitting, and asked him for help.

Carson gamely agreed and stood in the aisle to give a one-man show for more than an hour.

SHARP WIT

More service with a smirk: bringing snooty passengers down a peg or two is an urge some stewardesses cannot resist, despite rules about being pleasant at all times.

When one pompous woman passenger asked, 'And how is the domestic servant situation in England these days?' she was told, 'I'm sure you'll have no difficulty finding employment, madam.'

On another occasion a whining passenger had complained endlessly to the stewardess about her sore throat. Whenever the woman was offered medication she claimed that it was useless. Finally the stewardess appeared carrying a tray on which rested a carving knife.

BOTTOMING OUT

If you have ever spent a restless night thrashing about bag-eyed in an economy class seat trying to snatch some sleep, it might pay to travel business class instead.

British Airways market researchers paid volunteers £10 to spend the night reclining in test models of business class seats, to see how comfortable they were. The nine-hour stint, conducted in great secrecy at the Heathrow Park Hotel, was aimed at evaluating five different types of reclining seat. Results of the test, and the comments of the guinea-pigs, were not made public. Hmm.

BOUNCING BOMBS

An Australian airline staff magazine carried an article warning stewardesses of the dangers of having their breasts enlarged.

Air girls who had had silicone implants to improve their cleavage could find their implants expanding at high altitudes, it claimed.

'If air pressure in a plane changes suddenly,' the article stated, 'the silicone implant might expand like a balloon to two or three times its normal size, and the breasts might explode.'

Medical experts dismissed the claim as 'nonsense'. Though it would have made a rivetting change from the in-flight entertainment.

The nearest this cautionary tale ever came to reality was in 1967 when an American jetliner lost pressure over Los Angeles. One of the more dramatic results was a stewardess's inflatable bra which expanded to a creaking, drumskin tight 44 inches. In panic she whipped out a hairpin and deflated it before it threatened to strangle her.

MELTDOWN

Stewardesses might be trained to cope with any emergency but, at times, enthusiasm can go over the top. One girl spilled red wine on a businessman's shirt and kindly offered to wash it in time for his meeting.

She removed the stain successfully, but unfortunately decided to dry it out in the galley microwave. The passenger was very grateful, and deeply impressed, until he tried to fasten the buttons. They had all melted.

COVER-UP

If some passengers ever speculate what stewardesses might wear when out of uniform, British Airways Barbados manager Ian Pickup can offer a clue. He was forced to ban stewardesses from holidaying on the island from his office because they wore hardly anything.

'The style of dress varies,' he reported in the airline magazine, 'but the overriding theme is one of semi-nakedness.'

THE TAPE CAPER

In 1975 America's Federal Aviation Authority, in an exercise of mind-boggling pointlessness, spent $50,000 measuring air stewardesses.

The official excuse was that detailed measurements would help in the design of safety equipment. But the resulting 100-page report on the statistics of 423 air girls read like bureaucracy gone bananas.

Among the measurements, all carefully recorded, were 'the skinfold of the upper arm', the amount of slackness in each calf, the distance across the knees whilst sitting and several unique approaches to measuring buttocks from unusual angles.

Despite the inescapable conclusion that the whole exercise was some kind of raunchy practical joke, the Federal Aviation Authority carried it out with great solemnity.

OUT OF THE BLUE

Life in the air can be full of surprises. In 1984 Stewardess Susan Mackie made a one-night stopover in Quatar and thought she had a tummy bug. Shortly afterwards, in her hotel room, she gave birth to a baby boy.

'I was all on my own and I haven't any medical training,' she said at the time. 'It wasn't difficult. It was just natural.'

Her predicament was perhaps understandable. Dr Kathleen Draper wrote in *Mims Medical Magazine* in 1980 that international time zones often confuse stewardesses and make them forget to take the pill every twenty-four hours.

'Some stewardesses, wise after the event,' the *Sun* noted, 'carry a special watch giving Greenwich Mean Time.'

ANOTHER FIRST FOR B.A.

A steward on a British Airways 747 told the airline that he was having a sex change operation, and wanted to apply for a job as a stewardess.

The steward, said to be 'terrific with people', was given a ground administration job under the name of 'Vicky' while his request was considered.

A British Airways spokesman said, 'This is the first time in the history of the airline that this has happened. But the problem is being treated sympathetically. Our doctors are co-operating closely to ensure that the transition is a happy one.'

KEEPING COOL

Those cool-as-a-cucumber American stewardesses conceal a problem which has baffled medical science – the 'Red Sweat'. Not a problem peculiar to Soviet defectors, but a strange rash which breaks out among cabin staff.

It was first reported in 1980 by Eastern Airlines girls flying between New York and Florida. Pilots and passengers were unaffected by the sudden eruption of faces, hands and chests which lasted several hours.

Some of the sixty stewardesses who still suffer occasionally say that spots appear suddenly and give the appearance of oozing pink fluid. At one point their union threatened to ground planes unless a cure was found.

Stewardesses are certainly overworked – but sweating blood?

IT WAS THE BUTLER

For anyone seeking proof that the quality of in-flight movies has declined: in 1977 stewardesses at Heathrow would stand at the cabin door and say to passengers leaving the plane, 'Please do not reveal the ending of the film to passengers awaiting departure.'

A NIP IN THE AIR

A stewardess on a Caravelle flying between Ajaccio and Marseilles in 1969 was about to make an

announcement over the intercom when she let out a howl of horror.

A chilled silence descended over the passengers whose imagination raced through every permutation of disaster. The stewardess regained her composure and made an apology, explaining that she had been bitten by a live lobster carried on board by a Corsican.

COME UP AND SEE ME SOMETIME

One stewardess story, now something of a legend, concerns a girl who was being propositioned by two persistent Romeos, at opposite ends of the plane.

One of them was making strenuous efforts to get an invitation to her flat. The other was equally determined to persuade her to visit him. In a flash of inspiration she appeared to change her mind and asked the second passenger for the key to his apartment, promising to slip up and see him. She asked him to write down his address so that there would be no mix-up and, with a smile of anticipation, he scribbled it on a piece of paper.

The stewardess then walked to the other end of the aircraft and handed the key and paper to the other Romeo.

'Come up and see me as soon as you can,' she winked.

SERVICE CHARGE

No matter how rigorous the training, a stewardess making her first flight always finds something difficult to cope with.

In 1968 a Pan-Am girl was serving drinks and becoming confused about the exchange rates of the different currencies handed to her. In the middle of one transaction she found herself so hopelessly lost that she excused herself and took the dish of money to the lavatory to sort it out in peace.

In the middle of her calculations she was called away to attend to a passenger, accidentally leaving the money behind. It was some time before she returned and found, to her surprise, that the dish contained an extra $45 in change from passengers who assumed it was there for tips.

QUAINT CUSTOMS

Who can withstand that laser gaze when an extra bottle of duty free is burning a hole in your suitcase? Every overseas journey, eventful or otherwise, always ends in that hall of judgement, the customs sheds.

The green in 'green channel' is not as in 'go', but 'you must be green to think you'll walk out of here unscathed'.

British customs are, in fact, havens of tranquillity compared with some of their foreign counterparts. On entering the People's Republic of China, I recall a huge dustbin for depositing unwanted fruit before proceeding to customs. A travelling companion had his pockets turned out when a minute piece of orange was spotted, trapped in his front teeth, as he tried to smile disarmingly.

Worst of all are the Middle Eastern countries, where any sign of Western decadence is treated with great seriousness. Unwary British construction workers emerge from ferocious grillings with their copies of the *Sun* either mutilated with scissors or defaced beyond recognition by marker pen.

Here we encounter more strange Arab idiosyncracies ... the woman whose string of sausages were treated as high explosives ... and the vibrator that caused a bomb scare ...

PSST ...

It took several trips to Britain before a wealthy Chinese businessman realized why he had received an odd look from the Gatwick immigration officer the first time he entered the country.

'Have you any money?' the officer asked, scanning his passport.

The businessman glanced around furtively, and whispered, 'How much are you asking for?'

LIMP THIS WAY, SIR

'Customs officers at Cairo Airport discovered the director of a company that makes rosaries with 16 lb of hashish stuffed in his artificial leg.'
Daily Express, 1971

UNFORTUNATE CASES

Passengers playing the giant roulette wheel, otherwise known as the baggage carousel at New York's John F. Kennedy Airport, were distracted by the sight of a large suitcase with a split in the lid, and a human arm dangling out.

The unfortunate occupant was Audley Gibson, twenty-one, who had climbed inside in Kingston, Jamaica, and travelled with his brother-in-law's luggage to halve their air fare. The plan had failed to take account of the fact that baggage holds are unpressurized.

Michael Szweu, nineteen, worked on a similar scheme when he grew homesick for Australia after living in Philadelphia for six years. He constructed a 5ft × 4ft × 3ft wooden crate, labelled it 'Laboratory Equipment Machinery' and climbed in to mail himself back home.

Friends in New York lowered in two suitcases, a water container, sandwiches, copies of *Playboy* to read on the journey, a packet of cigarettes and a supply of travel-sickness tablets. Then they nailed him in and delivered him to the air-freight terminal at Kennedy Airport.

After thirty hours in a warehouse waiting for his flight, he became rather bored and called out, asking where he was, in the hope someone would hear him.

Police were called and pulled him out in the nick of time. Szweu, they said, would have died of cold or lack of oxygen if he had made the trip.

THE GREAT BUTTY HEIST

Night watchmen at Heathrow's high-security strong-room were surprised by six armed men who burst in and tied them up. They were even more surprised when the gang grabbed a particular package and fled. It contained the guards' sandwiches.

A PERSONAL ALARM

Baggage handlers at Calgary Airport, Canada, were offloading luggage from a Vancouver flight, when one of them detected an unusual humming sound from a suitcase.

The handlers fled from the tarmac and called the bomb squad, who promptly cleared the airport. Their first move, a standard procedure, was to pump compressed air into the case in the hope of detecting smoke, or triggering a controlled explosion.

When nothing happened, they gingerly approached the case and cut it open. Inside was a personal vibrator, whirring merrily after being jolted into action by the freight handlers.

TALES FROM THE ARABIAN FLIGHTS

The pilot who announced, 'We are now approaching Saudi Arabia, please put your watches back 600 years,' was not really joking.

Air travellers' tales from the Middle East often have an affinity to a 'Carry On Up The Desert' movie,

particularly at the hands of Saudi customs officials –
ever vigilant for traces of alcohol, pork, or pictures of
scantily-dressed women.

One ex-patriot housewife returning to Riyadh
opened her suitcase in the customs hall and was
mortified to see that her mother had slipped in a jar of
her favourite Fortnum's pork pâté.

The customs officer homed in on the offending
container, sniffed it suspiciously and demanded to
know what it contained. Driven by hysteria, and the
prospect of a lengthy visit to a Saudi jail, the woman
screamed with laughter and told him it was face
cream.

'It's to remove wrinkles,' she cried, slapping
handfuls of the precious pâté on her cheeks. 'See.
Wonderful, wonderful stuff.'

The customs officer watched, slack-jawed, as she
clicked her case shut and walked briskly from the hall
plastered in pâté.

A relative of mine was once arrested in a Middle
Eastern state for attempting to enter the country with a
bottle of Crabtree and Evelyn aftershave. The charge:
illegal possession of alcohol. The arrival of a junior
British consular official, freshly shaved and shimmer-
ing in a haze of *Old Spice*, did little to alleviate the
problem.

Long queues are common at Saudi Customs, as
officials thumb through family snapshots, magazines
or mail order catalogues for evidence of improper
dress or indecency.

The same relative thought he had seen everything until two very expensive first editions of Stanley's *In Darkest Africa* were whisked from his suitcase. To his undying horror they were returned from an office with all the engravings of African women inked out in felt-tip pen.

His wife had her collection of cassette tapes of ballet music similarly impounded. They were handed back with the legs of the ballerinas obliterated from the cover picture on each cassette.

BANGERS

Heathrow was placed on terrorist alert in 1983 when customs officers suspected an Italian woman of carrying dynamite strapped under her clothing.

When she was taken away to be searched, instead of high explosives they found sausages. The woman was on her way to visit relatives in New York and knew that sausages would not be allowed into the country, so she decided to smuggle them.

DANGEROUS CARGO

Security checks at Britain's airports reveal a growing number of bizarre and potentially lethal items people try to carry on board in their hand baggage.

A routine check in 1984 found one passenger carrying 144 quarter-litre bottles of hydrochloric acid. Four airline security staff spent four days in hospital after being exposed to the corrosive liquid and fumes.

In another incident an over-exuberant rugby player smuggled a paraffin warning lamp, taken from road works, full of highly inflammable fuel. When two jumbo jet passengers had their hand baggage searched, security-men found 960 disposable cigarette lighters. A further 163 lighters were found in their suitcases.

In one swoop on a single flight, no less than 2,500 fireworks were removed from the hand luggage of assembled passengers. To add to the mystery, it wasn't even bonfire night.

THE LEAST EFFICIENT BAGGAGE SCANNER

Security precautions at Middle Eastern airports are usually robust but, beneath all the show of efficiency, how thorough are they?

Not very, according to a reader of *Business Traveller* magazine who was flying from Madras to Heathrow in 1987. Over Kuwait, London contacted the captain to say there might be a bomb on board and he should land immediately.

A reception committee of police and firemen in asbestos suits was waiting. Everyone had to disembark and all the luggage was off-loaded. After several hours it was decided that there was no bomb on board, and passengers were ordered back onto their Air India flight.

'Before leaving the terminal,' the reader said, 'we had to file through a metal detector. After we had all passed through without a hitch, someone noticed a cable trailing across the floor. The metal detector had been unplugged the whole time.'

WELL, I DECLARE

A planeload of skiers returning from holiday were diverted from Manchester to Liverpool, where they disembarked to wait for customs. Unfortunately no customs officers appeared to be at the airport.

The families, tired and weary from the journey, were herded into a shed and locked in. Uniformed security-men stood guard as they watched through a glass-panelled door for the customs men to arrive.

Two hours passed and still no-one came to inspect their suitcases. There was growing discontent, punctuated by rousing cries of, 'Let's burst down the door and make a run for it.'

Security-men mustered uncertainly on the other side ready to repel a break-out. When they saw the fifty passengers grouping for action they backed down and opened the doors. The travellers collected their luggage and rushed for the exits.

A Customs and Excise spokesman said later, 'There is nothing I can say.'

BANG AND OLUFSEN

A business traveller on a domestic flight from Stockholm to Gothenburg, in Sweden, found that his bag had been loaded aboard the wrong aircraft.

'Unfortunately, security guards decided to carry out a spot check of the baggage on the other aircraft,' he told *Executive Travel* magazine.

Unable to find the owner of the bag, they called the anti-terrorist squad at the double to blow up the bag from a safe distance. The mistake was realized as the man's underwear, toothbrush and souvenirs floated down onto the tarmac.

SPOILING THE BROTH

There were heated scenes when some of the world's top chefs flew into Heathrow in 1983 for the International Gastronomic Festival.

The prestigious event drew master chefs who competed with each other for culinary supremacy. Understandably they wanted to keep many of their recipes and ingredients secret. Which explains why tempers frayed when they refused to reveal to customs men exactly what was in the pouches of herbs and spices they were carrying. It eventually became clear that they were not party to the drugs haul of the decade.

GIVEAWAYS

Customs men are noted for their lack of humour. So never take a leaf from Groucho Marx who was waved through by customs, only to waggle his eyebrows and say in a stage whisper to his wife, 'They've missed the opium, darling.'

They hauled him back and went through every piece of luggage for an hour.

For future reference, customs officers know how to spot the amateurs carrying that extra bottle of wine or carton of cigarettes.

'They tend to fidget,' says one officer. 'They sweat a lot and can't stop talking, usually with too much forced humour. They tend to involve their wives and children to distract us from asking them to open up. And often their eyes will swivel guiltily towards the suitcase with the extra drinks.'

You have been warned.

THE CASE OF THE FILTER-TIPPED CIGARS

Being harassed by customs is bad enough, but when they find something you had forgotten you had, it can be highly embarrassing.

Business Traveller magazine picked up the story of the couple who were taken to one side by over-enthusiastic customs officers at Madrid Airport. Acting on some ill-founded suspicion, the officers almost pulled their luggage apart.

Finally, one of the officers homed in on a box of Tampax and, convinced they were contraband cigars, shouted and waved them triumphantly above his head.

STEP THIS WAY, MISS

Stewardesses at Heathrow were furious that a crackdown on drug smuggling was being used by customs officers to ask them to strip naked for body searches. The invitations, according to British Airways, had got completely out of hand. Despite the officers' enthusiasm, no stewardesses were caught smuggling drugs.

PLANE DAFT

Considering the millions of people who fly each year, it is quite amazing that a proportion make determined efforts to leave aircraft in mid-air. Do they know something we don't? The reason, apparently, is that flying is a confusing experience. Some wake from fitful sleep convinced that they have landed and are late for an appointment. No amount of reasoning can persuade them otherwise.

Being on board an aircraft is rather like staying in hospital. Sitting there in plastic surroundings, there is little to do apart from wait for the next meal to come around. And, like patients, we generally do what we are told in the belief that it must be alright. A Belfast couple, as we shall see, flew to Bulgaria perched on what seems to have been an orange box next to the pilot.

Small wonder that amid the tedium of passing time travellers lose all sense of time and place. Like the elderly couple who changed into their nightwear and climbed into luggage racks thinking they were bunks.

The following stories are not tales of horror, or wild goings-on, but simply the unbelievably daft situations which arise once unsuspecting passengers step into the air travel system.

LAND OF THE FREE

In 1969 actor Justin McDonough decided to pass the time on a flight from New York to Miami by learning his lines. When the aircraft touched down, passengers were asked to remain in their seats.

The reason became clear when a squad of armed Miami police boarded the plane. The stewardess pointed at McDonough, shouting, 'That's the one.' The unfortunate thespian was promptly handcuffed and dragged away protesting his innocence.

A woman sitting next to McDonough had heard him struggling to master the lines of the Declaration of Independence, and had quietly alerted cabin staff that a revolutionary was muttering to himself 'about slavery, freedom and the necessity of overthrowing bad government.'

The pilot, taking no chances, had immediately called Miami ground control and demanded a reception committee.

THE MOST PREMATURE CASE OF HOMESICKNESS

A Rotherham man who had booked a package holiday to Bulgaria buckled himself into his seat for his first air trip – and minutes later had second thoughts.

As the engines whirred into life, he lost his nerve and, despite efforts to calm him, insisted on getting off. The pilot had to taxi back to the terminal building where the man almost fell down the aircraaft steps in his hurry to return to the safety of Rotherham.

SHOULDERS TO THE WHEEL

Most airports, for reasons of neat parking, prefer aircraft to come to a halt nose-in to the terminal building. Once the next complement of passengers is aboard, the pilot switches his engines to reverse thrust to back out and taxi to the runway.

Such was the position facing a thirty-seater Brown aircraft waiting at Leeds Airport in 1986 for clearance to leave for Glasgow. When the captain put the engines into reverse, there were a few violent shudders and shakes, but the plane refused to move an inch.

The embarrassed pilot was left with only one alternative. He walked through from the cockpit and asked the assembled businessmen, 'I wonder if there are any burly chaps who could give us a push?'

The businessmen, roaring with laughter, rolled up their sleeves and manoeuvred the plane away from the terminal. The perspiring team were rewarded with free drinks when they staggered back to their seats.

HAVE CASH, WILL TRAVEL

British Airways staff at the Concorde check-in desk thought they had seen most first-class idiosyncrasies, until a wealthy Arab traveller arrived with three bags stuffed with £800,000 in bank notes.

Their weight – exactly a hundredweight – meant that they could not be taken aboard as hand luggage, but would have to be stored in the hold. The Arab coolly solved the problem by immediately buying a £1,119 seat next to him for his bags.

CLUB CLASS

Cabin staff have been persuaded to allow on board items larger than the standard cabin-size bag. A passenger boarding an American flight to Florida asked if he could store his set of golf clubs behind the pilot's seat. Unfortunately, he found the precious storage space already occupied by someone's grandfather clock.

Staff had to draw the line, however, with an American who tried to board an aircraft carrying a 20ft-long carved pole, which he had bought as a souvenir from the Shetland Isles. When permission to stow it along the aisle was politely refused, he stormed back into the terminal carrying the pole, hit the entrance door, and snapped it completely in half.

UNDER STARTER'S ORDERS

One of the more amusing tales from the minefield of Middle Eastern air travel concerns the perennial problem of overbooking.

At one time the practice was so rife in Saudi Arabia that the only way to ensure a seat was to arrive at the foot of the aircraft steps before anyone else. Hence the 'Saudi Derby', a free-for-all of women, children and perspiring British businessmen haring across the tarmac, often before the incoming plane had rolled to a halt.

One aerospace executive, anxious not to offend local tradition, quickly entered into the spirit of things. For five consecutive visits to the Kingdom he was convinced that he was taking part in a colourful local custom of 'greeting the pilot'.

FLYING BY THE SEAT OF YOUR PANTS

The Balkans are famed for their colourful folklore and customs, but Bill and Eileen Laird discovered that the quaint traditions extend to air travel, too.

When they boarded their Russian Tupolev jet in Belfast, they found that their seats had been double-booked. The indomitable Bulgarian cabin crew were unruffled by such small technicalities. They ordered the Lairds to sit on a wooden box in the cockpit for the four-and-a-half hour flight.

The box, however, was barely big enough for one, and Eileen and Bill had to take turns to squat on it. Throughout the journey the pilot and co-pilot ignored them, as though their unusual seating was part of the normal accommodation plan.

'At first, Eileen sat behind the pilots, and I sat on the box in the corner,' Bill said. 'But she did not fancy the view so we swopped.

'The whole thing was incredible. I was terrified, and the landing, especially, was very frightening. The two pilots, though, did not seem to think it was at all unusual. It was as if this happened every flight.

'They hardly spoke to us at all, but the stewardess still brought in our meals and tea as though we were normal passengers sitting in normal seats.'

The return trip was just as eventful. Bill was told that there was no flight available for him. He had to wave goodbye to Eileen and follow her two days later, via Sophia and London.

THE PACKAGE HOLIDAY PIONEER

In 1922 the package holiday was in its infancy and suffering endless teething troubles. Booking and confirming flights could lead to the nightmares we are still familiar with today. None are quite as bad as the luck which befell a Frenchman who booked a holiday in Colombia, Central America, through the Workers' Travel Association.

The bracing outward flight went without incident, but perhaps only because enough trouble was piling up to fill the ensuing fortnight. As soon as he arrived, the Frenchman found that his hotel was overbooked. A little dismayed, he wandered the streets looking for bed and breakfast and was promptly arrested for vagrancy.

'Unwilling to bribe the police, he blamed the hotel when the magistrate heard the vagrancy charge,' says author Brian Moynahan, who unearthed the case. 'The magistrate was the hotelier's brother, and he sentenced the tourist to eight days imprisonment for slander.'

Because of his confinement he was unable to confirm his flight out of Colombia. 'By the time of his release,' says Moynahan, 'his return flight had left. He hadn't enough money to buy a scheduled ticket. He went to the post office to send a telegram to his home, asking for money. He was rearrested before he could send it. This time he was charged with illegal immigration.

'It was explained that, having missed his return flight, he could no longer be classified as a tourist. He now needed a work permit and did not have one.

'He was fined £250 for this offence and a further £250 for slander when he again blamed the hotel for overbooking him. His luggage was confiscated in lieu of the fines.

'Down to the clothes he stood in, he hitch-hiked to Bogota, the Colombian capital, where the consulate arranged his repatriation.'

Of course, it could never happen today – could it?

THE OVERNIGHT SLEEPER

In the days of early transatlantic flight, which now seem far removed from the endless roar of Gatwick, aircraft had large hammock-like luggage racks instead of the snap-shut lockers of today.

To the fascination of crew and passengers alike, an elderly couple changed into their night clothes and clambered into the racks under the misguided impression that they were overnight bunks.

STIFF PENALTY

Alarming false announcements might raise a few smiles after the event, but some people fail to see the joke. During an internal American flight a high-spirited passenger grabbed the intercom microphone and announced that the plane was about to make a crash landing.

One woman became totally convinced she was about to die and successfully sued both the prankster and the airline for $10,000 compensation.

HOW TO ATTRACT THE STEWARDESS'S ATTEN-TION

The image of the beautiful stewardess serving the needs of tired male travellers does not go down well with feminists who, at times, wonder what they have to do to get a simple glass of orange juice.

The answer was supplied by Maureen Pendered,

who wrote to the *Daily Telegraph* complaining that the worst treatment when air-travelling 'often comes from other women – glitzy receptionists and air hostesses conditioned to charm busy businessmen.'

Ms Pendered, from Redhill, passed on the advice of a woman friend whose employers fly her first class to assignments.

'Ignored yet again when the free juice and papers were handed out,' Ms Pendered wrote, 'she shouted down the aisle, "What do you have to do to get service on this plane – grow a penis?" Instant consternation. Instant service.'

THE LAST SUPPER

If, heaven forbid, you did find yourself plummeting earthwards in a stricken aircraft, would your life really flash before you? It seems not.

Ninety passengers were aboard a Boeing 727 over New Mexico when one of its three engines fell off. Thanks to the great skill of the pilot it landed safely. Waiting reporters asked one of the passengers for his private feelings in those final moments.

'I thought I was dead,' he said. 'And then I thought, "What a terrible last meal".'

ST TRINIAN'S TAKES OFF

Everyone had settled in for their in-flight meal as the aircraft flew at 30,000 ft somewhere between Florida and Cleveland.

A small child, making a loud fuss about eating, disturbed a man sitting behind him, who promptly complained to the child's parents. The affronted father replied by flipping a butter pat from his fork into the man's face.

The man, totally outraged, responded by grabbing a handful of food from his plate and throwing it at the father. Some of it landed on target, while the rest overshot and splattered passengers eating on the next row.

They reacted by throwing back portions of their own dinner which, in turn, missed and hit other passengers. Within minutes the cabin had erupted into a food fight with most of the 115 passengers taking part.

By the time the aircraft had landed the cabin walls, ceiling and passengers were plastered with food. There must have been a rule somewhere authorizing the crew to take action, but they were all too helpless with laughter to do anything about it.

WHAT A GAS

If you are dyspeptic and flying Pan-Am, there may not be too much relief at hand. The airline stopped distributing Alka Seltzer on demand because too many passengers took the tablets without dissolving them in water. The result of this unusual practice was explosive reports of what Americans call 'gas attacks', caused by decompression.

A BIT OF A CARD

The chore of filling in landing cards presents problems to some passengers. As a flight from New York neared Heathrow the British Airways stewardess went round the cabin collecting completed landing cards.

One American, however, was having problems. 'Ma'am,' he said, puzzled. 'It says here fill in the forenames. I've only got two.'

WHERE THERE'S A WILL

There was little to pass the time in the main economy cabin of a plane on an internal flight from Miami to Los Angeles. Little, that is, until the curtains leading to the first-class compartment were flung open by a blonde woman drinking from a champagne bottle. The most noticeable thing about her was that she wore a large grin, and nothing else.

She scampered down the aisle of the DC-10, eluding the grasp of pursuing cabin staff, and clambered over seats. The naked woman shook off all restraining attempts and perched on the top of a seat, guzzling from the champagne bottle.

As rows of bemused passengers craned for a better view, she shouted, 'I've just inherited five million dollars.'

Spontaneous clapping and cheering broke out. Even the cabin staff joined in, before wrapping her in a blanket and escorting her back to first class.

According to a passenger, 'she slept soundly the rest of the way to Los Angeles. But it was all too much for her travelling companion – he just crawled under a seat.'

An airline spokesman added, 'This was not part of our standard in-flight entertainment.'

The incident was more entertaining than the day in 1980 when Australian June Morrison, fifty-three, paraded down the aisle. She was said to smell of drink as she sang 'Waltzing Matilda' and picked her teeth with an army knife.

At Staines Magistrates Court, where she subsequently appeared after assaulting a passenger, Mrs Morrison explained that she had 'claustrophobia'. She was fined £750 and swore that she would never fly again.

EXCESS BAGGAGE

For the islanders of Tonga and Samoa in the South Pacific, physical perfection means tipping the scales at around twenty stone.

The average South Sea Islander is so fat that airlines are faced with an unusual problem. When flying at normal seating capacity aircraft are dangerously overloaded. Special rules now apply to certain Tongan and Samoan routes which require thirteen seats to be kept empty on Boeing 737s to remain within the safety limits.

Despite the Irish being a nation of potato-eaters, Aer Lingus do not normally have such problems. But they still recall the Dublin-to-London flight in 1967 which was grounded for an hour as stewardesses struggled to get a seat belt across the gargantuan stomach of their biggest passenger. When they admitted defeat the aircraft had to wait while ground crew installed an extra-wide seat.

As far as seating goes, the perennial oversized passengers are the walking wounded who hobble home from skiing holidays with broken legs in plaster and arms crooked in casts at shoulder height.

Three injured skiers prevented a flight from Munich from taking off in 1970 because someone dug out an international rule which said that if their broken legs were blocking the aisle, they had to occupy two seats.

Before the aircraft was given clearance, passengers had to embark on a complicated musical chairs manoeuvre with moves choreographed by shouting officials. According to one report, 'one girl wore a mini skirt and had great difficulty preserving her dignity while everybody heaved her leg about.'

DRESS: FORMAL

These days, it isn't enough just to have an airline ticket, you have to dress the part, too. What exactly the correct attire for flying is, no-one seems quite sure. But World Airways of America claim to have a pretty good idea.

Mr Donald Colgan and his wife Magdalena boarded a plane from Los Angeles to Frankfurt and, at a refuelling stop in Baltimore, were taken to one side by a supervisor.

They were told that their grey matching jogging

suits were considered inappropriate dress for air travel. The astonished Colgans, who had bought their tickets through a friend, had not seen the accompanying brochure requiring passengers to wear suits or sports jackets for men, dresses, skirts or trouser suits for women.

Anxious not to cause a scene, the couple asked for their luggage so that they could change. The airline refused and the plane took off without the Colgans, but with the Colgans' luggage.

THE FIRST LAW OF FLYING

The first law of air travel, as defined by the *Wall Street Journal*: 'The proximity of a screaming child to you in the aircraft will be directly proportional to the importance of the highly technical reading material you must digest for a crucial business meeting at your destination.'

Now there speaks a voice of experience.

A SLIGHT OVERSIGHT

In 1983 Martin Brown left his farm in Wood Eaton, Oxfordshire, for the trip of a lifetime. He had spent more than a year planning his six-month journey to Singapore, Australia, New Zealand, Fiji, Hawaii, Los Angeles and New York, and ploughed every penny of his savings into the journey.

The air tickets cost £1,150 and months had gone into arranging accommodation and obtaining the necessary visas. The only small point he had overlooked was that he had never actually flown before, and had no idea if he would enjoy it.

Mr Brown, twenty-two, was driven to Heathrow by his parents who waved him goodbye as he boarded the British Airways BA One-Eleven to Singapore.

When the 'fasten seat belts' sign came on, Mr Brown began to sweat. By the time they were taxiing and the stewardess was demonstrating the lifejackets and oxygen masks, he was shaking.

When the engines were approaching full power the pilot announced that they would have to return to the terminal because of an electrical fault. Suddenly, it was all too much for Mr Brown. When the gangway was wheeled back into place he hurried down the steps and did not return. His luggage went on to Singapore.

The unwilling passenger told the *Sunday Express*, 'There is no getting away from it. I got too frightened and panicked. Going to the airport I was more excited than nervous. But once I entered the plane fear took over. There was all this talk of oxygen masks, seat belts, lifejackets and emergency doors.

'I braced myself for take-off, gripping the arms of the seat tightly. Then, when the captain suddenly announced there was an electrical fault, it was the last straw. No words of comfort or persuasion from other passengers or airline staff could make me change my mind. Now I suppose I will never fly again.'

I'LL EAT MY HAT

A British Airways passenger, who appeared to be unhappy with his in-flight meal, protested in an unforgettable manner.

A message which was flashed to the airline's customer relations department before the plane touched down read, 'Apart from strange comments he was making to the crew, he took the stewardess's hat from stowage and ate it. Repeat, ate it – with no salt or pepper.'

WHERE THERE'S SMOKE

In these troubled times the growing antagonism between smokers and non-smokers can reach flash-point in the crowded confines of an aircraft. In one heated disagreement in 1979, the pilot was forced to land his airliner to stop passengers arguing among themselves.

On a crowded flight from New York to Washington, lawyer Richard Lent asked to be moved to the non-smoking section. When he was told that the non-smoking seats were full he pointed out that, under American law, every passenger had a right to sit in the non-smoking area.

'I'm sorry,' the stewardess apologized, 'but what can I do?'

'You can extend the non-smoking area right down to my seat,' the lawyer told her.

The stewardess thought about it, then agreed – to uproar from smoking passengers who suddenly found themselves in a non-smoking area.

The two factions, shouting loudly, stood up and began jostling each other in the aisle – smokers blowing smoke over non-smokers in protest.

As the row became more hostile, the captain announced, 'If passengers do not sit down at once, I will be forced to land at the nearest airport.'

At this there was pandemonium. Smokers and non-smokers became more hostile, pushing and threatening each other. Over the noise the voice of the captain told them, 'OK, you asked for it.'

He made a detour to Washington where the two sides were separated to cool off. To avoid further trouble, two planes were laid on for the rest of the journey to Washington.

The urge to light up can be overpowering. Mississippi businessman Steven Varvaris, for instance, enjoys a good cigar, but his smoking habit has earned him a jumbo-sized reputation.

In 1985 a TWA flight from Athens to New York was diverted to Heathrow for an emergency landing when he refused to put out a cigar. In the ensuing mêlée a seventy-seven-year-old woman collapsed and had to be taken to hospital.

Mr Varvaris, who is reputed to have been 'banned for life' by Delta Airlines, is particularly partial to eight-inch Irwin cigars.

The greatest craving for a cigarette was displayed by businessman John Johnson between Atlantic City and New York in 1986. He agreed to extinguish his cigarette when the steward asked him, but found the urge to light another uncontrollable.

Mr Johnson charged down the aisle of the Allegheny Airlines jet to appeal to the pilot. When he realized he could not be heard, he ripped off the astonished captain's headset and pleaded, 'I just have to have a smoke.'

Unimpressed by this pathetic interruption, the captain ordered him off the flight deck. To throw himself on the pilot's mercy, Mr Johnson grabbed the controls, sending the aircraft into a steep dive. It was only the intervention of two passengers who knocked him out that prevented a serious mishap.

ONE LUMP OR TWO?

An Arab claimed £15,000 compensation after a stewardess spilled scalding coffee on his most precious assets. The accident, on a British Airways jumbo, left him unable to make love for two months, his lawyers claimed.

The 'grossly negligent act' made him 'humiliated and embarrassed', they said. 'He suffered great pain and was temporarily unable to be involved in intimate physical relations.'

The incident, of course, was completely unintentional and reminiscent of the stewardess who knocked a gin and tonic over the trousers of a first-class passenger. She mopped him up as best she could, apologizing profusely, and brought him another gin and tonic. The stewardess then turned to leave – and knocked that one over him, too.

I DOOOO ...

A mystery man in a white dinner jacket hired a plane for a mid-air wedding and took off from Las Vegas with a public notary, to perform the ceremony, and a video crew.

At 10,000 ft, without saying a word, he opened the door and stepped out. After a day-long search of the desert below, there was no sign of him.

'He sort of opened the door and fell out,' said dazed public notary Charlotte Richards, who owns a Las Vegas wedding chapel.

Detectives investigating the strange incident thought it was suicide, but later began to wonder if it was something else. 'It might have been a publicity stunt,' one officer said.

Less spectacular, but only just, was the aerial wedding of cemetery millionaire Doc Williams and model Marian Sutton over Iowa. The idea was to duck the waiting period laid down by Minnesota law after divorce. To celebrate, a second plane drew hearts with vapour trails, and outlined 'just married' in skywriting.

A SCOT'S WHA' HEY

Passengers on a Monarch Airlines flight to Ibiza discovered the answer to the age-old question of what a Scotsman wears under his trousers.

After downing half a litre of scotch, a Glaswegian stood up and gave a practical demonstration. A stewardess fled to tell the captain, who diverted to Toulouse and handed him over to French police. The unscheduled landing cost Monarch £2,000 in fuel and airport fees.

A GNASHING OF TEETH

Apart from the unfortunate businessman who pulled off the lavatory door handle from the inside, there can be few episodes more sweat-inducing than that which befell a TWA passenger in 1976.

As the jumbo roared at 38,000 ft between Los Angeles and London, the unfortunate man went to the loo and caught himself very nastily in his trouser zip. After a long and excruciatingly painful struggle he realized that it was a no-go situation. In desperation he called the stewardess.

Despite her training, the girl was so taken aback that she rang for the steward. When neither could do anything to relieve his agony, the pilot was summoned. At Heathrow a doctor boarded the plane, armed with anaesthetic, a pair of pliers (for the zip) and a bottle of olive oil to help the operation run smoothly.

The man was eventually released and sent on his way, presumably never to venture into a jumbo lavatory again.

WHAT A COCK-UP

Back in the days of the Shah an American woman, Mrs Albert Brockman of Long Island, was among a diplomatic party landing at Tehran Airport.

She told Hugh Vickers, author of *Great Travelling Disasters* (Macmillan), of her embarrassment when her poodle, Gigolo, raced down the aircraft steps. The dog, which had loyally held its bladder throughout the flight, shot past the guard of honour and spent a penny against the Shah's imperial uniformed leg.

RING OF FORTUNE

In 1938, when some aircraft still had open windows, a diamond ring fell from a passing plane and hit Mrs Anna Briggs on the head. As a result of a personal column notice, she returned the ring to its owner and received a reward of £150.

A newspaper ran the story and syndicated it around the world. In the course of its travels it came to the attention of the German consular authorities who identified Mrs Briggs as the niece, and only surviving relative, of Andreas Subba.

Mr Subba had died in Germany many years before, leaving £25,000 to his relatives. All previous attempts to trace her had been unsuccessful.

TEST CASE

The old joke about 'breakfast in London, lunch in New York, luggage in Singapore' carries an uncomfortable ring of truth. Baggage handlers, who always claim to be overworked, do make mistakes. But what could happen if, suppose, they only had a single case to handle – they couldn't possibly lose that?

On one unique occasion it occurred and the answer, of course, is that they did.

When Derek Mayhew turned up for a flight from the Arabian Gulf to London he was surprised, and quite delighted, to find that he was the only passenger. Groups of Arab baggage handlers stood around idly with nothing to do but pick up his lone suitcase and place it in the hold of the 250-seat Tri-Star.

On the journey Mr Mayhew received possibly the

most prompt attention on record from a full staff of stewardesses.

When they touched down at Heathrow the hold was opened and found to be empty. The Gulf baggage handlers had forgotten to put his suitcase on the plane. Three days later Mr Mayhew and his luggage were reunited.

In terms of angst the story is possibly matched only by that of *Executive Travel* magazine reader Simon Calder who had his luggage searched in Bucharest in 1985.

More precisely, the Rumanians wanted to search Mr Calder's luggage, but it had already been loaded aboard the aircraft. They therefore asked him to sit in a waiting room until the plane had flown to Brussels and on to London, then returned via Brussels to Bucharest. When his suitcase was finally unloaded, officials looked through it and allowed him on his way.

THOSE MAGNIFICENT MEN

The secret of successfully piloting an aircraft is evidently to believe at all times that you have done everything right. This was brought home to me on a scheduled flight to a small airport in the Deep South.

On landing, the plane seemed to drop from about six feet above the runway, bursting open luggage lockers and generally throwing everyone around in their seats. When we came to a halt the pilot announced in an Alabama drawl, 'Ladies and gentlemen, the safest part of your journey is now over. Drive carefully.'

Pilots do have a sense of humour, albeit a difficult one to penetrate. It appears to verge towards practical jokes at the expense of unsuspecting passengers, such as asking them to steer the aircraft with lengths of string while the pilot goes to the lavatory.

Perhaps it provides a release from the pressures of the job. Stress is common among the wind-tanned men of the skies resulting, as we shall see, in bizarre behaviour. The pilot who believed he was a dog ... another who thought he was God (though this may not come as a surprise to some cabin staff) ... and the captain who became so fed up that he simply landed in some foreign field and walked away from it all ...

But, with some of the passengers they are obliged to suffer, who can blame them?

GOOD LORD

Catholic pilgrims on a packed Aer Lingus flight to Lourdes had their meditations interrupted by a message from the pilot over the public address system.

'You Catholic bastards, stop the rosary,' he barked, to a rather stunned silence.

The captain, who had intended the announcement as a private flight-deck joke, had no idea that the intercom had been left switched on.

It was only when a passenger, Canon Patrick Murray, rose from his seat and stumped down the aisle to tackle the offender that the horrified pilot realized his error.

The Irish priest returned with an apology. 'I believe in forgiveness,' he said.

Aer Lingus, however, took a different view. The captain was suspended pending the outcome of an inquiry.

IT'S A LOCK-OUT

Cross-country flights in Nigeria tend to be informal affairs. The captain of one aircraft making the 250-mile hop from Lagos to Port Harcourt liked to socialize with his passengers en route.

When the flight was under way, he switched to automatic pilot and left the controls to wander down the aisle, chatting to familiar faces and welcoming newcomers.

Unfortunately, half way through his rounds, the aircraft hit a pocket of turbulence and lurched unexpectedly. The steel anti-terrorist door between the passengers and cockpit slammed shut, leaving him stranded.

A wave of anxiety rippled down the aircraft as the pilot, smiling reassuringly, attacked the lock on his hands and knees with a plastic spoon from the galley. It was rather like trying to open a bank vault with a bent hairpin, but everyone shouted encouragement.

The nerves of some passengers could stand no more as he laboured gamely. After a hurried conference a group of them shoulder-charged the door with a force motivated by such undisguised fear that it was torn completely from its hinges.

CHAIN-SAW MASSACRE

It may be reassuring, or otherwise, to learn that most United States pilots do not die in aircraft crashes. According to a survey, the most frequent cause of unexpected mortality is chain-saw accidents.

FLIGHT-DECK DINING – A SYSTEMS APPROACH

So many knives and forks find their way behind aircraft seats when passengers disembark that ground crews now use powerful magnets to retrieve them. The reason for this, it seems, is that if enough of them accumulate, the pilot can find his compass navigation seriously impaired.

To test the theory, Captain Ron Bridge of the Guild of Air Pilots and Air Navigation Safety Committee, took compass readings from the control panel of a

Boeing 737 as he tucked into a hot meal with a magnetized knife and fork.

Each time he raised his fork to his lips, the compass moved one degree off course. If a pilot was ill-bred enough to eat from his knife, Bridge found, the compass swayed wildly out of true by up to 20 degrees.

Despite the alarming results, copies of Debrett's *Etiequette And Modern Manners* have still not been distributed to air crews.

SLEEPY-TIME TALES

Not that we should worry unduly, of course, but a report by the Institute of Aviation Medicine in 1985 does provide restless reading.

A two-year study of pilots revealed that more than 100 of them repeatedly mentioned tiredness as a daily problem. And about a dozen actually confessed to falling asleep at the controls.

One expert, Dr Roger Green of the investigation unit Confidential Human Factors Incident Reports, thought the situation 'less than satisfactory'. Passengers should perhaps be alert to stifled yawns echoing from the intercom.

The Civil Aviation Authority tend to take pilot fatigue very seriously. One captain who feigned loud snoring noises over the passenger loudspeaker system as a practical joke was severely reprimanded.

Off the major traffic routes, sleepy pilots are not unusual. At midnight, a BBC director chum found himself stranded at Georgetown Airport, Guyana.

Despite having chartered a jet to fly to Trinidad, he was told by an airport official, 'Sorry, everyone's in bed – we're closed.'

Incredulous, the BBC man stalked the empty runways until he found his aircraft hidden behind a hangar. After hammering on the door of a nearby hut the pilot emerged, rubbing his eyes, and complaining like a London cabbie.

'Look mate,' he complained, 'I've been to Trinidad twice today, Venezuela once – that's my lot, I'm going back to bed.'

Half an hour later, after a great deal of persuasion, the pilot reluctantly agreed to take his lone passenger. The BBC man climbed abaord while a teenage co-pilot, who obviously knew little about flying, settled into the control seat. The pilot promptly fell asleep next to him.

As the aircraft trundled uncertainly down the runway, the captain opened one eye and slapped the youngster violently on the wrist.

'Don't touch that knob,' he shouted. 'I told you never to touch that knob.' And slumped back into sleep again.

DON'T LOOK NOW, BUT …

Lance Stirton, a passenger on a twelve-seater commuter aircraft flying to Sydney was taking in the view over the Pacific when something distracted his attention. No-one else aboard the 300-mph jet had apparently noticed the pilot hysterically waving his arms around.

Curious, Mr Stirton walked along the aisle to the flight deck to find the captain slumped face down over the controls. He hauled the officer back into an upright position and, in some alarm, tried to figure out how to use the radio.

After a few fumbling attempts, Mr Stirton contacted a voice which identified itself as Sydney air traffic control. Passengers by this time were gathering in the doorway in a state of anxiety.

Sydney Control explained in a reassuring voice how to check if the plane was flying on automatic pilot. When Mr Stirton and a chorus of passengers confirmed that it was, there was an audible sigh of relief from the loudspeaker.

As Sydney issued instructions on how to land the aircraft, Mr Stirton worked desperately to revive the pilot who, he was convinced, had had a heart attack.

A few minutes later, as pandemonium reigned, the pilot opened his eyes, shook his head and asked: 'Where am I?'

When the circle of nervous faces blurted our what had happened, the pilot told them, 'Even with the best help in the world, I don't think you could land this aircraft …' And, with that, his eyes began to close again.

Mr Stirton put an oxygen mask over the officer's face and, after several heart-stopping moments, he began to show signs of reviving. The captain recovered to make a perfect landing in Sydney. An ambulance waiting on the tarmac rushed him to hospital where his mystery illness was diagnosed as food poisoning.

ALARMING DISCLOSURES

Flying an aircraft can be an alarming experience – especially for a pilot confronted by up to fifteen emergency warning devices which can suddenly emit a variety of heart-stopping noises.

The Medical Research Council's applied psychology unit at Cambridge has tried to sooth the jangled nerves of flight-deck crews by inventing a 'calm alarm'. The device plays a dulcet melody to replace the more ear-splitting klaxon effects pilots are used to. If an engine falls off, they can presumably nod along in time to the music.

MOVE ALONG INSIDE, PLEASE

Britain's travelling businessmen have suffered the best, and worst, of airline idiosyncrasies. One of their favourites, voted Worst In-Flight Announcement in *Business Traveller* magazine, concerned the British Airways captain preparing to take off from Faro in Portugal.

'I wonder if we could have some volunteers to move up and fill the front seats,' he announced, 'so that we don't scrape the tail on take-off.'

When the aircraft touched down, his keenness to get everyone off became apparent when he told passengers that the last one to leave would have to stay behind and clean up.

PLANE CRAZY

The stewardess made her way among the passengers dispensing meals when, without warning, the flight-deck door burst open to reveal the captain advancing towards her on all fours. He stalked down the aisle, barking like a dog, and bit the embarrassed stewardess on the leg.

It was not a practical joke, but just one example from the strange casebook of Professor Lionel Haward, professor of clinical psychology at Surrey University. In 1982 the prof. published an article in the medical journal *Stress Today* about the odd behaviour of pressurized pilots.

Among his reports of sky-high crack-ups was the pilot who suddenly threw his Boeing 707 full of passengers around the skies as he tried to dodge imaginary Japanese anti-aircraft flak. He had to be knocked unconscious by cabin staff to enable the co-pilot to take over.

Then there was the skipper who decided he could not face another flight. He made an unscheduled detour to a strange airport and walked off, never to be seen again, leaving all his passengers stranded.

And, perhaps most amazing at all, there was the pilot who failed a routine flying inspection and vowed to seek revenge by dive-bombing the examiner's office. The official, says Prof. Haward, was extremely lucky to survive the kamikaze attempt.

'The pilot killed himself, but not the intended victim, whose bliss in an adjacent white-tiled salon was rudely shattered by the explosion. Rarely has a penny proved so providential.'

The professor's research, on at least one occasion, extended to stress suffered by passengers. He recalled the story of a pilot who died in mid-flight, leaving passengers with the problem of landing.

They pinned their hopes on an elderly man who had a vague recollection of six flying lessons he had had as a teenager. He remembered roughly what to do with the controls and managed to communicate with air traffic control, who asked him to read his instruments.

They issued simple instructions and, miraculously, all went well until the crucial landing approached. The man's running dialogue with the control tower suddenly dried up and stress overwhelmed him. He was struck totally dumb, until an inspired fellow-passenger had the brainwave of forcibly pouring whisky down his throat to relax him.

'He landed,' says Prof. Haward,' drunk but alive.'

NO STRINGS ATTACHED

The classic flying story, which has now been transformed into legend, concerned the captain of a transatlantic American jet who emerged from the flight-deck looking worried.

He exchanged words with a stewardess who announced, 'Would any good drivers aboard make themselves known to the captain immediately.'

A few minutes later the passengers' worst fears appeared to be confirmed when the pilot backed cautiously from the flight-deck, gingerly holding two pieces of string attached to instruments on the control panel.

Fighting to maintain a straight face, he then handed the strings to a passenger on each side of the aisle, and asked them to take over while he went to the toilet, explaining that if they pulled too hard the plane would bank to the left or right.

With the aircraft safely on autopilot, he then disappeared into the galley to stifle his mirth.

WHITE KNUCKLES TO FRANKFURT

A story similar to the above also passed into the annals of in-flight folklore, but fortunately there are witnesses to verify it.

Passengers were glancing at their watches, ready to depart from London to Frankfurt, and grumbling quietly because the pilot was late arriving. His seat, visible through the open flight-deck door, was clearly empty and there was no sign of him.

The most vociferous passenger was a German businessman, sitting on the front row, who kept demanding to know where the captain was. Five minutes later he was threatening the stewardess, 'If he doesn't show up soon, I'll fly the damn thing myself.'

British passengers, most of them publishers bound for the Frankfurt Book Fair, exchanged smirks and settled behind their newspapers. They quickly lowered them a few minutes later when the German, now furious, stormed into the flight-deck, thrust the headphones on and began pulling and pushing every control in sight.

Uncertainty set in among the passengers. There was a tense silence, and white knuckles on the armrests as the plane began to taxi to the runway. The publishers, with true British aplomb, did not say a word.

The aircraft roared into the wide blue yonder and a voice came through the tannoy, 'This is your captain speaking. Tomorrow I retire. Sorry to give you a scare, but I've waited twenty years for the opportunity ...'

HERE'S A GOOD PLACE TO PULL OVER ...

Tales have been told of pilots tapping their way to the flight deck with white sticks, or studiously reading copies of 'Elementary Flying Techniques'.

Among the most common reported japes are the pilots and co-pilots who leave the intercom deliberately switched on while a rapt audience eavesdrops on horrendous recollections of mid-air near-misses, or suicidal urges brought on by marriage break-ups.

Beneath those cool exteriors, it seems that the world's airlines abound with pilots who are pent-up practical jokers. Sometimes it can go a little too far.

For the benefit of passengers who are still awake, captains often make an announcement when they are flying over the Swiss Alps. In good visibility the peaks can be seen peeping through the clouds.

One pilot, however, could not resist taking it further. Thirty thousand feet above Switzerland, he announced that the Alps could be seen below, and added, 'Let's go down and take a close look at the scenery …'

The jet dipped alarmingly, sending at least one half-consumed gin and tonic flying, along with countless hopes of ever returning safely. The aircraft levelled out and the captain's voice said, 'Not to worry, just my little joke …'

At least he knew where he was. One passenger who asked if his wife could visit the flight-deck en route to Paris was shocked to find the pilot poring over a tattered motorist's map, of the type sold at filling stations. It was, of course, all a joke. At least, that's the way it was explained to her later.

DON'T BLAME ME, COMRADES

There is nothing to match the urbane, unflappable tones of a British captain issuing reassuringly from the tannoy. Often he will apologize for a delay, even when

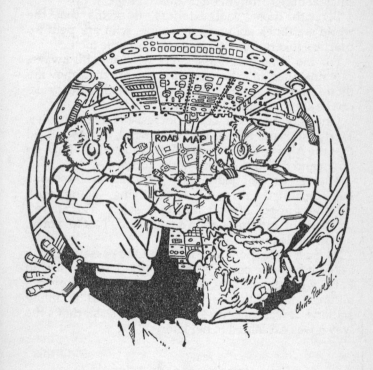

the fault is clearly out of his control.

In Russia things can be rather more testy, it appears. A correspondent of the Soviet newspaper *Pravda* was delayed for more than two hours aboard an Ilyushin 62 at Moscow Airport. As the passengers became increasingly restless, the loudspeaker crackled to life and the pilot shouted, 'I am NOT going to apologize to you. We pilots are NOT to blame. We are here because of the negligence of the airport workers.'

Having unloaded that from his chest, he added, 'The weather is fine and the plane continues to be ready for take-off.'

OH DEAR, WHAT CAN THE MATTER BE?

As 300 New York-bound passengers prepared to board a TWA jumbo at Heathrow, they could hardly have imagined that their crew, tired and bedraggled, were shouting for help through a restaurant letter box.

The bizarre situation happened in 1985, when the co-pilot and flight engineer decided to have a late meal in an Indian restaurant in Kensington before take-off.

At the end of the meal the two crewmen decided to go to the toilet as the last customers were leaving. When they emerged after a wash and brush-up, the place was deserted. All the lights were out and the front door was locked.

As passengers began to check in, the crewmen desperately hammered on the restaurant door to attract the attention of passers-by. Alas, it was London; hours went by and no-one answered their pleas.

Finally, as they chorused for help through the letter

box, a passing policeman heard them. He contacted the manager, who turned up with the keys at 7 am.

When the pair arrived at Heathrow they were declared unfit for duty because they had been awake all night and had not had the regulation rest period.

LOW-DOWN PEEPING TOM

On a hot summer day in 1982, university student Susana Lawson was sunbathing in a deckchair in her garden when a strange shadow passed over her.

She looked up to see a plane criss-crossing low above her head 'ten or eleven times'.

'I was wearing a swimming costume,' said a puzzled Mrs Lawson, of Grange-over-Sands. 'I'm an ordinary woman without any stereotyped female attributes. Perhaps there was another lady sitting in the garden next door – I don't know.'

The aircraft circled so low that she noted its number and complained to the Civil Aviation Authority.

BUZZ OFF

An American pilot, flying at 8,500 ft, settled back to open a piece of chewing gum. When half the stick was in his mouth a bee landed on it, and he spat the gum out in shock at the windscreen.

The bee, he told *Flying* magazine, was not very happy and circled for an attack, joined by another bee. The pilot lashed out at them with his chart and the bees countered with a low level ascent up his trouser leg.

In total panic he radioed the nearest control tower to make a hurried landing. When the aircraft came to rest in front of the wire perimeter fence, the pilot leapt wildly out and dropped his trousers – to a burst of applause from a passing patrol of Girl Guides.

HICKORY DICKORY

No-one is quite sure how it happened, but a mouse found its way into the cockpit of a plane en route to Alaska in 1983.

In a search for a warm and comfortable sanctuary it scampered up the pilot's trouser leg, found itself in a cul-de-sac and started to nibble its way to freedom.

According to one aviation spokesman, 'the startled pilot shot out of his seat and started dancing around. The rest of his shocked crew thought he was going bananas.'

In what will probably stand as the all-time fastest in-flight sprint record, the captain ran to the passenger lavatory and dropped his trousers. In the heap of crumpled clothing a three-inch, angry-looking mouse stared defiantly back at him.

In Delhi they take no chances. When the crew spotted a mouse on board in 1985, the flight was cancelled. Two hundred passengers were put up in an hotel for twenty hours while pest control officers scoured the aircraft.

CLOSING TIME

We tend to think of airports as beacons of bustle, pulsating twenty-four hours a day. Nothing, it seems, could be further from the truth.

In 1985 a Dan Air jet, delayed by bad weather, made its approach to Aberdeen carrying sixty passengers. Just thirty seconds from landing it was forced to overshoot the runway because the airport staff had locked up and gone home.

The plane had to land 150 miles away at Glasgow as Aberdeen is forced to close at 10.30 each night because of noise restrictions.

'We feel pretty sour about it,' said a Dan Air spokesman.

'We sympathize,' said Aberdeen, 'but the law is the law.'

A pilot found himself in similar straits over Blackpool when his twin-engined aircraft was left circling for thirty-five minutes in 1983 because the air traffic controller had closed the office and gone home.

The plane, on a return flight to Belfast with Sunday newspapers, had to fly around until another controller was brought to open up the tower.

'The controller went home thinking the flights had finished,' said an airport spokesman.

OH DEAR, WHAT COULD THE MATTER BE ...?

Beyond the ultimate disaster, it's probably the worst fear of every air traveller. A businessman on the

Birmingham-to-London shuttle went to the lavatory and, when he tried to get out, pulled the door handle off in his hand.

The embarrassed man was taken short, appropriately, aboard a Shorts 330 aircraft.

The pilot appealed for a screwdriver, but it proved too small to loosen the door knob screws. As the struggle to free the businessman continued, a fraught awareness dawned on the faces of the other passengers. No-one would be able to use the loo until they touched down at Heathrow.

He was freed when the aircraft landed, and promptly fled into the terminal to cover his embarrassment.

'We would like him to get in touch with us,' said a British Midland spokesman, 'so that we can offer him some sort of recompense. Even if it is only an embossed toilet roll.'

DON'T BLAME ME

The British Airways morning flight to New York touched down at Heathrow in September 1986 with a great thud, followed by several judders and a squealing of brakes.

As passengers recovered their composure the captain announced, 'Welcome to London, ladies and gentlemen. I hope you enjoyed most of your flight, and I apologize for that rather ropy landing ... by the first officer.'

HIGH-FI

A personal stereo may be better than the battered headsets handed out on long-haul flights, but more disturbing for the pilot.

The Civil Aviation Authority has been warning of the risk of hi-fi equipment sending navigation instruments haywire since 1972. It's a case of when the electronics go west, everyone could find themselves going east.

Soon after the guidelines were issued a transatlantic jumbo strayed seventy miles off course when a passenger turned on his personal hi-fi. The error was only discovered when he switched the set off. So never play 'Fly Me To The Moon' – the on-board computer might take you literally.

THE EQUALIZER

When a pilot was called to deal with an offensive passenger in September 1987, newspapers mercifully kept his identity secret.

The Captain's technique was unusual, to say the least, but very effective. A stewardess complained that she had been harassed and pestered by a drunken hooligan who ignored her requests to be quiet.

The pilot, a muscular six-footer, made his way down the aisle brandishing a fire axe and confronted the trouble-maker. According to one reliable report he inserted the blunt edge of the axe under the offender's chin and lifted him bodily from his seat.

As he hung there, wide-eyed, the captain warned, 'If I have any more trouble with you, I'll eat you.'

The flight proceeded without a murmur.

KNOCK, KNOCK

The cabin crew had done everything to prepare for the morning flight from Heathrow to Bangladesh. The no-smoking signs were on, the doors were firmly closed and all the passengers had their seatbelts fastened.

As the stewardesses prepared for the safety demonstrations, there was a knocking from outside the fuselage. They tried to ignore it and smiled reassuringly as they had been trained to do.

The knocking, according to one passenger, became louder and more frenzied until someone had to do something about it. A stewardess cautiously opened the door to see who was outside – and, with an embarrassed smile, in climbed the pilot.

THE £150,000 TAKE-OFF

When Captain Reuben Ocana found himself diverted from Shannon because of fog in 1983, he realized that he was running out of fuel.

His Gulfstream executive jet, en route from New York to Munich, could not reach another airport before his reserves ran out, so he radioed for help. Air traffic controllers directed him to the only flat piece of Ireland within range – Mallow racecourse.

Thanks to his skill the aircraft touched down safely – and there it stayed, bogged down to the wheel hubs in mud caused by the wettest May Ireland had experienced in 184 years.

The four passengers continued their journey by scheduled airline, and Captain Ocana and his crew were left with the problem of taking off again.

Lloyds of London mulled things over for two weeks without making progress, until someone suggested building the Gulfstream its own runway.

The boyos from the blackstuff were brought in to construct a 3,200-ft long, 36-ft wide take-off strip alongside the five-furlong straight at Mallow. As they worked, laying hardcore ready for a one-and-a-half inch layer of tarmac – total cost £150,000 – Captain Ocana recalled his unexpected landing.

'It was the most difficult moment of thirty-five years of flying,' he said, 'I was looking for somewhere without cows to land, and there are an awful lot of cows in this country.'

Weeks later, with £7 million insurance in case anything went wrong, Foxtrot Oscar Uniform took to the skies again.

A DREAM OF A FLIGHT

Alabama surgeon Dr Clayton Davie was piloting his Piper Cheyenne to Florida in 1985, when an overwhelming tiredness swept over him. The aircraft was on automatic pilot flying at 18,000 ft when Dr Davie dozed off.

When routine radio contact failed to raise him, air traffic controllers rang the US Air Force. Within minutes fighters were scrambled in hot pursuit.

The jet pilots roared around the still-sleeping doctor, hoping the noise would wake him, but were unable to fly too close in case turbulence disturbed his autopilot. After forty minutes' snoozing, the doctor awoke to find two jet pilots waving frantically to him alongside.

'I don't know how I went to sleep,' he said later.

NICE LANDING, WRONG AIRPORT

It was a clear, sunny morning and the pilot of the early Sabena flight from Brussels radioed Manchester for permission to land on visual control.

He lowered his wheels and flaps and lined up the 737 for a perfect landing. At the last moment an urgent voice came over his headset: 'Don't land, you're at the wrong airport.'

With seconds to spare, the pilot lifted off again, realizing that he was at British Aerospace's Woodford factory, not Manchester International Airport.

It was not the first time the mistake had been made. When the factory staged its own airshow an American pilot gave a flying display and finished with a spectacular fly-past at Manchester, instead of Woodford.

In the 1960s Northolt Airport was frequently mistaken for Heathrow. To make matters more confusing, each airport had a nearby gasometer. One 707 landed on Northholt's tiny runway in error, and could not take off again. Ever since, Heathrow's gasometer has been painted with the giant letters LHR (London Heathrow) and an arrow pointing in the right direction.

PLANE LUNACY

The trouble with piloting an aircraft is that you have little idea what kind of nutcases are sitting back in the passenger cabin.

A man left his seat on a flight from Washington to Montreal, stepped onto the flight-deck and, without a word, switched off the throttles and fuel supply. As the aircraft went into a steep dive, the man tried to intervene as the pilot struggled with the controls.

'Get him off my back,' the captain shouted. Women passengers screamed and through the windows the ground and trees could be seen coming up fast.

Another passenger, Professor John Henderson of Boston University, saved the day by knocking the man out. The pilot managed to regain control with just 200 ft to spare.

'The professor,' said one survivor with admiration, 'has a very strong right-hand punch.'

The heart-stopping incident was matched only by a charter flight from Palm Beach, Florida to Washington. The aircraft had been in the air just a few minutes when the thirty-five-year old woman who had chartered it punched the pilot.

Worse was in store when she turned to the co-pilot. 'Do you love me?' she demanded hysterically. With a mental agility that probably saved them all, he gave a nervous smile and said, 'Of course I do, baby.' At this, the woman fell on him and, in the words of an airline spokesman, 'alternately kissed and mauled him'.

The poor man managed to distract her with his attentions while the pilot turned the aircraft round and broke all speed records back to Palm Beach.

THE SINGED HANDLEBAR SYNDROME

There are still some airline pilots around the world who favour the waxed handlebar moustache pioneered by the RAF.

Word has it that the handlebar has become something of a handicap. One case in point was that of an airline captain who experienced a sudden loss of cabin pressure. He issued a warning to passengers and grabbed his oxygen mask but, as he put it on, to his astonishment his moustache burst into flames.

The pilot was left with the dilemma of trying to extinguish it with one hand, while wrestling with the controls to land his aircraft safely. The reason, according to one expert, was that oxygen accelerates combustion when it comes into contact with a greasy substance.

A journalist read the report and, concerned for his readers, rang the British Airline Pilots' Association. 'Haven't seen a waxed moustache in years,' he was told. 'They are much more popular with the French.'

A remark which should help us all to narrow our choice for future air travel.

STRAP HANGING

A pilot approaching Tetboro Airport, New Jersey, was studying his instruments and lining up for his approach when a tremendous banging erupted outside the fuselage.

As the noise became louder and more frenzied he began to sweat from head to toe, glancing out of the cockpit to satisfy himself that the wings were still on. With his heart pounding almost louder than the racket outside, he radioed for an emergency landing on any runway.

Flying magazine, which reported the hair-raising tale, said that he taxied to the control tower to be greeted by three yellow official cars. The serious-looking aviation officials broke into broad grins when they saw the pilot's seat belt hanging out under the door.

GROUND SICKNESS

Stress causes strange things to happen in the air, but one pilot found it hard enough to cope on the ground.

A story was leaked to the *Daily Star* about a pilot who went berserk at the controls of a flight simulator in the Midlands. He screamed, 'I've had enough of this,' then ripped off his clothes and locked himself naked in the lavatory. Security staff had to smash down the door and put him in an ambulance.

'Thank God it happened on the ground,' said a colleague, 'and not while he was flying over a housing estate.'

One can't help but agree.

PREPARE FOR NOD-OFF

As a footnote to the stories of pilots snoozing at the controls, Dr Martin Moore-Ede, of America's Harvard Medical School, came across some interesting case histories in 1986.

Among them was the story of the airliner which

over-flew its destination, Los Angeles, and ended up 100 miles over the Pacific because the pilot, co-pilot and navigator had all nodded off. Ground controllers had to activate chimes in the cockpit to wake them up.

Dr Moore-Ede investigated another incident in which an airliner flew off course into Canadian airspace while its two pilots slept peacefully. They were woken by the sound of defence fighters scrambled to intercept them.

In 1977 the whole flight-deck crew of a BOAC jet dozed off because of overwork. The pilot found himself nodding off at the controls as he flew 125 passengers to the Far East. He shook himself awake and saw his two co-pilots fast asleep. Then he looked over his shoulder and found the flight engineer asleep as well.

'I immediately called for black coffee to bring everyone round,' the captain reported. 'We were just tired out.'

For anyone interested in re-timing their flights after digesting this, half the incidents which came to the doctor's attention occurred between 3 am and 7 am

HELLO, HELLO

When pilot Bill Williams set off from Barton Aerodrome, Manchester for the Isle of Man in 1973, he ran into problems with low cloud. To play safe he landed on a remote, deserted beach on the Lancashire coast and made a long trek to the nearest phone box to report his position to the Civil Aviation Authority.

When he returned the only sign of life was a lone policeman, notebook in hand, examining his Piper Tri-pacer.

'Can I see your licence, sir?' the officer asked.

Captain Williams later confessed, 'I could hardly keep my face straight. At first I thought the constable was joking.'

When he explained that his documents were in Ghana and might take some time to produce, the policeman muttered something into his personal radio. The answer from HQ came back loud and clear: 'Book him.'

The pilot stood in stunned surprise while the officer wrote out a traffic ticket. The form solemnly stated that he was not a learner driver, and that the incident had not taken place on a motorway.

THE DAY JOB

Pilots have become an insecure bunch in recent years. Several small airlines have collapsed, creating a pool of unemployment, in addition to the risk of being grounded by six-monthly medicals and routine examinations.

Not surprisingly some take 'day jobs' and actually earn more from their second jobs than from flying jumbos. Jim Zockoll, the man behind Dyno-Rod, was a Pan-Am 747 pilot who unblocked London drains at £4 a time as a sideline. His moonlighting blossomed into an international franchise and propelled him into the millionaire bracket.

Pilots run chicken farms, travel agencies, factories building fibre-glass yachts and, in the case of Captain Sydney Brown, investment portfolios. In 1973, 200

BEA pilots were each chipping in £15 a month with a promise to take nothing out of the fund until they finished flying. They owned land in Malta, flats in Spain and shares in scores of companies.

The man up front with the gold braid may be more gilt-edged than we could ever imagine.

Conversely, there are those with mundane jobs who yearn to fly. Among them was George Leeper, a Dorset milkman, who applied for his pilot's licence in 1979 at the age of seventy-seven. Clearly a pensioner with a lotta bottle.

UNTIMELY DEPARTURE

Fifty-three passengers aboard a KLM DC-8 flying from Amsterdam to Tokyo in 1966 had no idea how close they came to disaster. As the aircraft was coming in to land, 150 ft above the runway, the pilot collapsed from a heart attack.

With seconds to go the co-pilot grabbed the control column and took the plane to 3,000 ft. After switching onto automatic pilot he made a perfect landing. Six hours later he was on the flight-deck for the return trip to Amsterdam as though it was all part of a day's work.

PLEASE CAN I HAVE A GO NOW?

Co-pilots are in the Catch-22 position of having to keep up their flying hours to retain their licence, but having little opportunity to take the controls.

Perhaps the most extreme case was British Airways

co-pilot Nigel Wood who was dismissed for having insufficient flying experience. His log book showed that between January 1972 and January 1973 he was at the controls of an aircraft for only fifteen minutes.

As a result, he was given an adverse report at his training examination. Mr Wood said, 'It was rather like taking Yehudi Menuhin's violin away from him for a year then asking him to play a concerto.'

CRASH COURSE

A Texas flying school promises a pilot's licence in just three weeks – if you are prepared to pay more than £2,000 and work day and night for it. Accidents are surprisingly almost non-existent, though there have been some hairy moments.

'We had one girl who got a little lost on her solo cross-country run,' said tutor David Millar. 'She radioed in that she was approaching a lake. We discovered it was the Gulf of Mexico and told her to turn round.'

THE BIG KICK-OFF

When three rowdy amateur football leagues boarded a Britannia Airways 737 at Manchester for a holiday in Palma, the pilot anticipated trouble.

To get them off the aircraft he announced that there were technical problems and everyone would have to return to the terminal. Inside the airport, 71 out of the 129 passengers were ordered home, and three who refused were arrested. The captain returned to the runway with a peaceful complement of passengers.

HIGH JINKS

Next time you try to squeeze that over-large grip under the seat and find it won't fit, and the locker is too small to accommodate it, don't despair. In the league of oversized cabin luggage you are definitely in the lower division.

Among the giants of bare-faced cheek are the man who wheeled two lorry tyres aboard, and someone who actually managed to disguise a corpse as personal luggage.

Flying can turn out to be an adventure even if you are the unlikeliest Indiana Jones. Like the unassuming Frenchman (is there really such a species as the unassuming Frenchman?) who threw air traffic controllers into a panic when he went to the lavatory … or the overbooked passengers forced to sit on each other's laps for take-off.

Then there are the out-and-out extroverts who see flying as one great ego trip. Luckily they are seldom as flamboyant as the man who believed he could step outside and defy the laws of gravity. But never judge too hastily – you never know when vanity is waiting to strike.

A publisher friend was aboard an American plane which was forced to make a dramatic emergency landing. Television news crews were waiting by the time the pilot made his final approach. When the aircraft came to rest the emergency shutes were activated. Passengers waiting to slide to safety could see the TV lights through the cabin windows. And more than a handful fixed their hair before emerging, then smiled as they whooshed towards the cameras.

MIND OVER MATTER

The most determined attempt to jump from an aircraft with no thought of a parachute was made by hypnotist and stage psychic Paul Goldin 1979.

He announced his intention – to the horror of the Civil Aviation Authority – of throwing himself from an aircraft and, 'with thought projection techniques to slow down my descent so that I will float to earth and land safely.'

Goldin got as far as boarding a private aircraft at Ipswich, Suffolk, but was grounded by gale-force winds.

Undeterred, he booked a second flight the following day, only to be told he would have to wear a parachute.

Goldin eventually agreed, but warned, 'There is nothing in the rule book to say I have to pull the cord once I jump out of the plane.'

At this, the Civil Aviation Authority panicked and hauled him off. As he was led away, Goldin shouted, 'These people have no spirit of adventure. I tried using my psychic powers on them, but their minds were closed.'

As he was ejected from the airfield his final words were, 'I'll make this jump somewhere if it kills me.'

IS IT A BIRD ...

Pilots and passengers flying up country in Botswanaland are generally ready for most eventualities, but few have had the experience of being attacked by a vulture.

Whether the bird was desperate for a mate, no-one will ever be sure, but one passenger told the following nightmare story to Hugo Vickers, author of *Great Travelling Disasters*.

The creature, sucked to high altitude by clear air turbulence, took out its misfortune on the aircraft wing, biting chunks from it as passengers peered through the portholes in terror.

They lined the windows shouting, 'Shoo – go away,' but it continued to ignore them. After demolishing a large portion of the wing with its razor beak, the vulture turned its attention to the fuselage, attacking the thin bodyshell with renewed vigour.

As passengers recoiled, it tore a hole in the side of the aircraft and popped its head in, eyeing the terrified bunch with a beady look. At this point the aircraft had taken as much as it could stand.

The pilot managed a forced landing in the jungle. Passengers and crew were found uninjured by local tribesmen who led them on a twenty-mile yomp to civilization.

The bald-headed in-flight entertainer was never reported again.

TO SAY NOTHING OF THE UNDERPANTS ...

The least that can be said about flying is that it is full of surprises. Sabena, the Belgian airline, at one time carried signs announcing, 'Live vest under your seat.'

STOP THE PLANE – I'M GETTING OFF

A British tourist flying to Toronto thought the plane had landed and tried to open the door – 34,000 ft over

Labrador. Passengers and a flight attendant dragged him back to his seat, but welder Leslie Campbell of Glasgow fought back, convinced they were trying to stop him disembarking.

Police, who later charged him with mischief to private property, said that he was 'not drunk or otherwise impaired', just determined to get off.

THE RELUCTANT TRAVELLER

As passengers on a British Airways flight from Bermuda to London tucked into lunch high over the Atlantic, they were puzzled by a strange knocking under the floor.

One or two left their seats to investigate and distinctly heard a voice crying, 'help'. The crew prised up the lavatory floor and found Sterling Smith, twenty-three, a Bermudan baggage handler, staring at them thankfully.

He had been overcome by tiredness while loading suitcases into the hold, and had accidentally dozed off on the job. The closing of the baggage hold doors failed to wake him and he slumbered on throughout take-off.

Mr Smith climbed out and continued the 6,000-mile journey with the other passengers. He returned on the next flight with a £298 bill for the air fare.

HARD LABOUR

Loganair's air ambulance, which operates around Scotland's remote islands, is generally ready for any emergency. Pilots, and nurses from Glasgow Southern

Hospital who staff the service, know however that when a patient is pregnant, anything can happen.

Sister Helen Kennedy recalls one mercy flight on which a pregnant woman in labour instinctively threw her hands behind her head whenever she had a contraction, and grabbed the pilot in a piercing grip.

Before he could adjust to this unusual behaviour, the woman had another contraction, and grabbed his arm with paralysing strength. The Islander plane went suddenly into a sharp dive as the agonized captain fought to prise himself free. It was only with the help of nurses and the woman's husband that he was eventually released to level-off the controls.

'All of us on board got a terrible fright,' Sister Kennedy said. 'After that, I had to ask the woman's husband to grab her hands every time she had a contraction.'

OUI, MON CAPITAINE

The *Sun* summed it up with its usual succinctness: LOO LA LA. FROGGIE'S WEE HITCH DELAYS JET, it chortled in 1987.

Roughly translated, a British Airways pilot was forced to abandon his landing at Heathrow because a French passenger was contemplating in the lavatory.

As the Boeing 707 approached London, the 'fasten seat belts' sign flashed on and the passenger made a last-minute dash to answer the call of nature.

'Unfortunately, his preoccupations took him longer than he thought they would,' an airline spokesman explained later.

Aviation rules clearly state that all passengers must be strapped in for landing. As puzzled air traffic controllers demanded to know why the aircraft could not make its approach, the pilot had to tell them, 'We can't land, someone's in the toilet.'

The plane circled Heathrow waiting for developments, while the captain told his passengers, 'We apologize for the inconvenience.'

The Frenchman emerged red-faced to a deafening roar of applause from 140 people. Five minutes later the plane touched down safely.

'At first we were all alarmed,' a passenger said, 'but when we realized the problem we couldn't stop laughing.'

ALL IN THE LINE OF DUTY

When it comes to flying, British businessmen have probably seen the lot and, if they survive to tell the tale, their exploits often end up in the well-thumbed pages of *Business Traveller*.

In 1987, 'routine' flying experiences included a Kenya Airways plane which took off with the forward door still open. The stewardess reassured everyone by covering it with blankets.

A Nigerian Airways flight leaving Lagos was overbooked, leaving three extra passengers with nowhere to sit. Stewardesses asked them to squat on the lap of the nearest passenger until after take-off, when they would be free to 'walk around'.

And finally there was the Singapore Airlines plane which was asked to circle the control tower at Kuala Lumpur before landing 'so that the authorities could see whether it was the owner of a wheel found back at Singapore Airport.'

JUMP JET

A single flea, no bigger than a match head, grounded a jetliner for twelve hours in 1983.

When it bit an Olympic Airways stewardess on the leg, the aircraft was immediately taken out of service and fumigated. The following day it was allowed to leave Heathrow for Athens with 200 bona fide passengers. The flea, said a spokesman in defence of Greek pride, was Egyptian.

CHOKED OFF

Henry Moore happened to be enjoying a martini on a flight home to Tucson, Arizona, when his wife Arleen leaned over and planted him with a surprise kiss.

Mr Moore was so startled that he swallowed both the olive and the cocktail stick. He began choking so badly that the aircraft had to jettison 1,500 gallons of fuel and make an emergency landing at Omaha.

Local surgeons managed to remove the obstruction, but Mr Moore was reported to be a little nervous when his wife, sitting at his bedside, said she wanted to 'kiss him better'.

THE LAST STRAW

All those big straw donkeys, beloved of Costa Brava tourists, have been banned by many airlines, along with Grecian urns and Spanish guitars.

On some charter flights the aisles were stacked high

with them, creating safety hazards. But European holiday souvenirs are in the small league compared to the extra cabin baggage American travellers try to take on board.

At one point the list of goods became so mind-boggling, and cabin staff so fed up that their union, the Association of Flight Attendants, complained about passengers breaking the rules.

We are not discussing the odd carrier bag, or over-large grip, but items such as an embalmed body zipped up in a garment bag and hung on the cabin coat rack. Or the woman who walked unsteadily down the aisle with a dog hidden beneath her hat.

'The popular definition of carry-on luggage is broad,' Dermot Purgavie of the *Daily Mail* reported. 'It seems to mean anything that can be raised without the assistance of a fork lift truck.'

According to Federal Aviation Administration records it has included two full-size truck tires, a stained-glass window, a stuffed rabbit which was so enormous it had to sit next to the pilot, assorted grandfather clocks, big-screen TV's and microwave ovens by the dozen.

Travel agent Reuben Flores found the answer in 1984 when he sent a stuffed bull as a paying passenger on a 1,000-mile trip to his sister in Newark, New Jersey. By buying the bull a seat, rather than sending it air cargo, he saved £100.

Perhaps the question is not how passengers manage to get such strange objects aboard, but what on earth they want them for. One British traveller is still puzzling over the two Pakistanis who boarded his plane in Karachi after each checking in a tree trunk as baggage to the United Arab Emirates.

JET LAGGARDS

Everyone has his own favourite recipe for beating jet lag. Few of them work, and the one to be avoided is perhaps most frequently recommended – a pill to make you sleep away the flight.

There is the cautionary tale of the businessman who liked to pop a sleeping pill into his mouth as soon as he fastened his seat belt, and sleep like a baby across the Atlantic. The method worked fine until his aircraft reached the main runway at Heathrow and had to turn back because of an engine fault.

When passengers were asked to transfer to another plane, cabin staff could not wake him up. He had to be carried on a stretcher, with his briefcase on his chest, to the replacement aircraft.

Researchers at Leeds University psychology department claim that sleeping pills actually leave travellers 'like a zombie'. Tests revealed that some are unable to remember things which happened only minutes earlier.

Dr Ian Hindmarch, from Leeds, reported in *Science and Business Link-Up* that international businessmen lose travellers' cheques, crash hire cars and muff important deals because of the wrong pills.

One woman volunteer admitted in the tests, 'I boiled two eggs, but forgot to put water in the saucepan.'

Is the future of Britain's exports in safe hands?

EXECUTIVE STRESS

There was some consternation when a TWA flight from Heathrow to the USA was overbooked in 1985. One British businessman managed to secure himself a seat, stowed his belongings in the overhead locker, took off his shoes and sat down with relief.

He noticed a spare seat and it occurred to him that he might be able to hold it for a colleague who had been left stranded in the terminal. The businessman asked if he could leave the aircraft for a minute to tell his friend there was a place available.

'He returned a few minutes later,' *Executive Travel* magazine reported, 'to find the 747 closed up and about to start taxiing – with his shoes, wallet, passport and luggage inside. Banging frantically on the door got him back aboard.'

The story smacks of the angst suffered by a WAAF girl towards the end of World War Two who happened to be sitting astride the tail of a fighter, cleaning it, when the order to scramble went out. The pilot took off, realized his error, and hurriedly landed again with the girl still clinging to the fuselage.

SWEET CHARIOT

A friend has never quite forgotten the old lady who took a flight from Liverpool's Speke Airport in the 1950s. Soon after take-off the stewardess circulated among passengers offering them barley sugar.

'What this for?' the old lady asked suspiciously.

'It's in case you have trouble with your ears,' the stewardess replied.

Without further ado the elderly passenger took two sweets, and stuck one in each ear.

The story is absolutely true, though it must be said that the same friend was once flying on a night operation to the Middle East. When the Hermes had refuelled at Malta and was on its journey again, he happened to notice a strange phenomenon. He peered through the window into the gathering darkness and nudged the soldier sitting next to him.

'Don't say anything,' he cautioned, 'but that red light out there has been keeping pace with us since we took off.'

His companion looked anxiously out of the cabin window and replied, 'You bloody fool, that's the end of the wing.'

ECONOMY CLASS RETURN

One of the world's most arduous flights is the long haul from Ascension Island to the Falklands. Standard accommodation is hard seats on a noisy RAF Transport Hercules.

Mrs Thatcher, on her much-publicized trip to the Falklands, is said to have been spared the indignity suffered by normal passengers. Air Force legend has it that a Portacabin was bolted into the Hercules to provide comfortable seats and home comforts.

Regular travellers must have found some consolation in the story of the return flight. Apparently the 'de luxe' Hercules was grounded because of technical problems, forcing Britain's First Lady to fly home in the manner of the hoi polloi.

FELLOW TRAVELLERS

Among the strange flying experiences of British businessmen in 1985 was the man on a Sudanese flight who found himself squashed into the corner of his seat by two large women and a live goat.

On another trip, according to *Executive Travel*, a stewardess apparently had an off day and bit the troublesome son of an American lady passenger.

Then there was the anguished memory of another executive who reported, 'On a Delta flight, I found myself sharing a seat with a man whose wicker lunch basket contained a rattlesnake which he fed twice between Dallas and Atlanta.'

The fine tuning of foreign culture is, of course, a major stumbling block to international understanding. Like the reader who pressed the call button for the steward when the man next to him began to moan and appeared ill. The steward patiently explained that he was a Muslim carrying out his prayer ritual.

My own favourite, probably because I have also witnessed it, was the man who 'watched helplessly while his seat companion, who had been given a hot towel, first looked mystified, then proceeded to clean the cabin window with it.'

Less amusing was the hapless executive in 1987 who spent the whole flight next to a lady clutching an urn containing the ashes of a dead relative.

MUSICAL BEDS

Japanese Airlines decided to make their service more appealing in 1978 by introducing sleeping accommodation on 100 aircraft.

It seemed a good idea at the time, but no sooner had the service started than passengers were climbing into each other's beds. Stewardesses were so appalled by the licentious goings-on that they all went on strike to demand higher standards of decency.

The girls claimed to be particularly unnerved by the sight of naked male passengers asking for drinks to be brought to them.

I REMEMBER WHATSHERNAME

Octogenarian Dr John Follows left his Dorset home in 1984 to visit his daughter in South Carolina. Unfortunately, by the time he had reached Kennedy Airport, New York, he could not recall her name or address.

Sadly, the good doctor decided that the best thing to do was to return. After a stay of just two hours he caught a flight home again – unaware that his waiting daughter had called in the police to search for him.

John Coker, an American en route from Detroit to Frankfurt had a similar experience at Easter 1979. After changing planes at Heathrow he found himself flying back across the Atlantic, instead of on to Germany. The unusual bank holiday outing was blamed on a Pan-Am check-in girl.

I'M FURIOUS – FLY ME

Now and again an airline pilot's normally cool composure can erupt in a furious row with his crew.

Passengers normally know nothing of this silent fighting but, when it causes a flight to be delayed, exposure is inevitable.

In 1972, for instance, a BEA One-Eleven jet bound for Geneva stood for two hours on the tarmac at Manchester while the captain and steward went at each other hammer and tongs.

The argument, allegedly because the steward was late on board, resulted in three of the cabin crew walking off the plane in sympathy. A replacement crew were called in but, because of the heated atmosphere, they decided not to fly, too. The plane finally took off with a new pilot and a third cabin crew.

For sheer dramatic quality, however, the incident paled before a row on the Heathrow-to-Glasgow shuttle in 1981. The first inkling passengers had was when the plane was taxiing to the runway. The captain announced over the public address system that he was returning to the terminal because of 'a disagreement with a member of the cabin crew'.

The aircraft was delayed twenty minutes because the captain wanted his sausage and bacon breakfast before the steward collected the walk-on fares. The steward told him he would have to wait, so the pilot promptly returned for a replacement steward who would serve his breakfast immediately.

There was a similar bacon-rasher row in 1978 when the pilot of an American scheduled flight from San Diego to Seattle was told that the last hot dinner on board had just been served to a passenger.

The captain immediately fell into a furious mood and made a public announcement that the aircraft would be making an unplanned landing at San Francisco to 'resupply'. When the jumbo touched down he stormed off to a restaurant for dinner and returned later to resume the flight to Seattle.

A SUDDEN LACK OF PRIVACY

In 1962 the door blew off an Allegheny Airlines plane over Connecticut. The sudden decompression sucked the toilet door from its hinges. Only the stalwart efforts of two male passengers prevented the startled occupant, twenty-two-year-old Katherine Lacy, from being taken with it.

THE BALLAD OF AUDREY BUMGUARD

A Texas oil driller with the remarkable name of Audrey Bumguard became the world's most celebrated bottom-slapper in 1977. His antics on a flight from London to Miami resulted in him being charged with air piracy.

Patti De Woody and Jane Otto, two stewardesses employed by National Airline – motto: 'Take me, I'm yours' – were serving drinks at the time.

'I thought he had had a few before boarding,' Miss Otto told the court. 'When I served him I poured out only a little of each drink. I had a feeling he might be a problem.'

Miss De Woody was slapped four times, almost

falling over on one occasion. 'I told him each time, "Cut that out",' she said, 'and he mimicked me.'

Miss Otto was slapped three times on the backside and complained to the pilot who warned Bumguard to stop. 'But shortly afterwards,' said Miss Otto, 'I felt another whack on my behind and I had to turn round and confront him again.'

Bumguard told the FBI, who arrested him at Miami Airport, that he had patted one of the stewardesses 'maybe once or twice'. He was fined $500 for what the prosecutor referred to as his 'rear action'.

After suffering such heavy-handed treatment it is no surprise that some stewardesses resent being projected as sex objects in airline advertising. When Continental Airlines of America promoted the slogan, 'We really move our tails for you', in 1975, five stewardesses tried to sue the company for £2 million. They claimed the slogan had resulted in harassment, obscenity, insults and other indignities.

Continental, whose previous slogan had been, 'Fly the proud bird with the golden tail', said, 'Flight attendants are valued and dedicated members of the company. We would never seek to denigrate an employee in any way.'

WINDY WEDDINGS

Ever since man took to the air the thrill of flying has brought out in him something of the show-off – a trait which has found expression in the strange desire to be married in the sky. Despite careful planning, airborne nuptials are not without their drawbacks.

One of the earliest, in 1897, was the wedding of Miss Cynthia Kenna, of Tennessee, and a rodeo rider, known simply as Robertson. Friends held onto the guy ropes of a tethered balloon while they exchanged vows inside the basket.

When the ceremony was over, they released the ropes to allow the happy couple to soar romantically into the blue. At least, that was the plan. The balloon shot upwards with such speed that Mrs Robertson, her bridal gown filling the basket, had difficulty keeping her balance.

As they approached 100 ft she lost her nerve and jumped into the Tennessee River. Her stranded husband, ascending at an even greater rate of knots, was left to watch as wedding guests hauled her from the water, dripping but unhurt.

By 1938 air travel held fewer terrors. An American couple, Marjorie Klinger, eighteen, and Donald Babcock, twenty, decided to get married in a plane and then parachute to earth to be greeted by their friends and relatives.

The ceremony went without a hitch and the couple jumped out at 2,100 ft. In her excitement at finally being married to the man of her dreams, the new Mrs Babcock completely forgot to pull the ripcord for the first 1000 ft of her descent. She remembered at the last moment and landed rather uncomfortably. The best man, following closely behind, was so distracted by the drama that he narrowly avoided plunging into a cement mixer.

Which brings us to 1950 and the tangled legal problems encountered by Miss Frances Warren, a stewardess, and her pilot fiancé, a Mr W. Scott. They were at Le Touquet, waiting to deliver a new company aircraft together to Bahrain, when they asked another pilot, Captain David Last, a complete stranger, to resolve a family problem.

Captain Last said, 'Mr Scott came up to me and said, "I want an air pilot to marry me in the air". He was with Miss Warren and a woman relative. I gathered from Mr Scott that the relative had heard of their intended flight and had objected because the couple were not married.

'I had never met any of these people before, but I've always been willing to help a fellow out of a spot. We took off in Scott's plane and the woman relative came too.

'I put all the usual questions – "Do you take this man as your lawful wedded husband?" – and all that. And then I asked Mr Scott to put on the ring.'

At 10,000 ft above the Channel Captain Last shouted into the intercom, 'Everything's fine. You're officially married.' He entered their names in his log book, noting that the ceremony lasted two minutes twenty seconds. Back in England, however, there was uproar as lawyers and marriage law authorities claimed that the union was illegal.

'I do hope there is not going to be too much of a fuss about this,' said Captain Last. 'After all, when a fellow pilot is in a bit of a spot, one generally does all one can to help.'

The happy couple, on their way to Bahrain, had other things on their minds.

FLIGHT OF THE BUMBLE BEE

Passengers on an airliner flying from London to Amsterdam in April 1949 had to share the journey with four million bees, packed in 150 crates.

Soon after take-off from Amsterdam, the 30-cwt cargo decided that it did not care for air travel and preferred to fly under its own steam. The bees found a gap in one of the crates and hundreds were soon buzzing around the passengers cabin. Travellers swung into action, rolling up newspapers and swotting at anything that moved. Soon there was a pitched battle between passengers lashing out in all directions, and bees zooming in for the attack.

After what seemed an eternity the plane landed at London, where cargo handlers were driven into an office by the swarm. One airport official was stung three times on the forehead. Another fled to an office when one flew up his sleeve. He managed to lock himself in the room with hundreds of bees, and spent thirty minutes swotting them with files.

Pilots have almost come to grief grappling with nature wild in tooth and claw. In 1960 a private plane flying over Picardy, France, had to make a crash landing when a flock of wild geese set upon the aircraft and forced it down.

The most ambitious ground-to-air attempt was by a timberwolf, annoyed by an aircraft flying low over snow-covered farmland in Minnesota. The wolf sprang into the air, gripping one of the plane's landing skis in its teeth, and hung on. The sudden imbalance caused it to crash into a snow drift. The plane was wrecked, but its two occupants were unharmed. The wolf disappeared, presumably in search of a dentist.

The human equivalent of this chance-in-a-million happening was caused by a Brazilian *gaucho* in the late 1950s. Furious that a low-flying survey plane was frightening his cattle, he reacted by throwing his lasso at it. The rope caught round the propeller and was dragged from his hands. The aircraft clipped the tops of nearby trees and crashed. Fortunately the pilot escaped uninjured.

CAUGHT WITH THEIR PANTS DOWN

The lure of the Mile High Club has given the famous, and the not-so-famous something to boast about. Those who have been caught red-handed – to say nothing of red-faced – may feel it wiser to forget.

A thirty-nine-year-old holidaymaker and his girlfriend slipped into the lavatory of a Dan Air flight from Rhodes to Gatwick, in 1985, to make love. As they came out the stewardess noticed a cigarette in the Romeo's hand and cautioned him for smoking in a restricted area.

He was fined £170 by Crawley Magistrates. As for the Mile High Club claim: 'He wasn't there long enough to qualify,' the stewardess said.

A married couple were arrested after a sex session on an American Airlines flight from Zurich to Chicago.

They had oral sex while other passengers slept, but were spotted by a teenage girl who woke her mother.

When a stewardess ordered them to break it up, two middle-aged peeping Toms, who had been watching the performance, pelted her with food and drink in protest. The couple were charged with public indecency when the plane landed. The two men were accused of disorderly conduct.

An Essex girl, on the fourth day of her honeymoon, had not had a chance to be alone with her new husband until they were on a flight from England to Cyprus.

The first three days had been spent with in-laws, but finally they were together on a VC-10 heading back to the RAF base where they both served. To celebrate they slipped hand-in-hand into the lavatory for a love session. It lasted so long that passengers had to bang on the door to ask them to hurry up.

When they emerged, both of them had completely forgotten that on RAF aircraft all seats face the back. The entire cabin faced them with broad grins as they filed back to their seats together.

TAKE ME TO CUBA

Skyjacking is not a funny business, as the pioneers of sky piracy discovered. They perished, along with the passengers, when the Catalina flying boat they had tried to take over crashed on its way to Hong Kong in 1948.

But even anti-terrorist experts admit that there have been occasions which have raised a smile. On one of them an Arab ate his in-flight dinner then held up the pilot with his knife and fork.

As the plane droned on to his demanded destination, tiredness and the effects of a full meal settled over him. The would-be hijacker nodded off and was quietly disarmed. He awoke in America to find that the plane had landed and he was wearing a pair of handcuffs.

SHRINKING FROM DUTY

In the early 1970s, when skyjacking almost rivalled skateboarding as the sport of the decade, there were various secret moves to arrest the problem.

Among them was a scheme which American aviation officials would probably prefer to forget. Airlines hired psychiatrists to build up detailed profiles of typical skyjack suspects for the benefit of security staff.

When the operation was in its infancy, one company posted two psychiatrists clandestinely at a New York

check-in gate to study passengers' behaviour. Before the day had passed, one shrink had been fallen upon by security-men and dragged away under arrest. The other psychiatrist had spotted his odd behaviour and reported him.

THE EASIEST HI-JACK ON RECORD

In 1976 an armed hijacker boarded a plane in New York and, as soon as it was airborne, pulled out his gun and jabbed it into the nearest stewardess, who later reported the following conversation:

Hijacker: 'This plane is gonna fly me to Detroit.'

Stewardess: 'That's right, sir. This is the scheduled flight to Detroit.'

Hijacker: 'Oh, good. Very good …'

And he returned to his seat and put the pistol back into his pocket.

A LITTLE LIGHT READING

According to an American handbook – *Everything You Need To Know Before You're Hijacked* – copies of *Playboy* and *Penthouse* in the hands of passengers drive religious Middle Eastern terrorists to violence.

Among the tips included in the book are not travelling on narrow-bodied jets because hijackers prefer them and, if you are a man, sit next to the window to avoid being pistol-whipped. The weeks between January 16th and February 11th are a favourite for Iranian extremists, it seems.

So, if you have a penchant for reading *Playboy* in an aisle seat, always wear a crash-helmet.

TROUBLE AND STRIFE

In 1982 a Sri Lankan villager, Sepala Ekanayake, hijacked an Alitalia Boeing 747 with 261 passengers aboard because he had split up with his wife.

In exchange for the passengers' safe conduct he demanded that she should be returned to him, along with a ransom of £300,000. Ekanayake was flown home with his wife and the money, and went on a five-day shopping spree before the outraged airline applied pressure to the Sri Lankan government to arrest him.

BEASTLY HIJACKERS

Hijackers are usually portrayed as desperate characters brandishing a gun and a ransom demand but, on occasions, birds and beasts have attempted their own kind of take-over ...

A Vanguard was grounded at London Airport in 1964 by a persistent sparrow. Despite the usual pre-flight checks, no-one had noticed the tiny bird doggedly building a nest in the space between rudder and tail-plane.

An air traffic controller spotted twigs and wisps of straw as the plane prepared to taxi, and immediately halted it. A scaffolding platform was rushed across the tarmac and a mechanic scrambled up to remove the debris which could have interfered with the rudder movement.

The platform had been removed and wheeled back when the tower reported that the sparrow was hastily stuffing twigs back into the same opening. Again the scaffolding was pushed out and nest material removed.

As soon as it was wheeled away the sparrow returned and began frantically rebuilding its nest. The game went on for more than an hour until mechanics pulled out the last of the debris, moved the platform clear and stood guard while the Vanguard made its getaway.

Transporting animals can be hazardous. The first lion to take to the air was caged behind the pilot of a Napier D.H. in 1926 as he made a nerve-racking hop from London to Paris. The cage on that occasion remained intact – others following in his flightpath have been less fortunate.

In 1966 three wild lions were flown from Ethiopia to Longleat aboard a Dart Herald cargo plane. Unknown to the pilot, the packing agents in Addis Ababa had built a cage with wooden bars – a mere snack to the king of the jungle.

Captain Paul Wurhman first noticed something unusual when he felt 'something warm and wet' snuffling around his feet. He turned to find three very hairy and unexpected passengers on the flight-deck.

As the co-pilot tried to drive them back with a fire axe the pilot made an emergency landing at Brussels. The aircraft had to be covered with nets as police and a lion keeper from the local zoo tried to coax them through the door.

There was more mayhem than terror when a British transport plane was forced to make an emergency landing at Orly. More than 300 monkeys on their way from London Zoo to Brindisi broke out of their packing cases and took over the aircraft. When the plane landed, two unsuspecting ground staff opened the doors to see what was wrong and were engulfed by chattering monkeys.

BY THE SEAT OF THEIR PANTS

Theoretically, the Wright Brothers should take most of the blame. Their first bouncing flight, no longer than the wingspan of a modern jumbo, made the world a smaller place. There were other pioneers, such as the early balloonists who landed themselves in a terrible mess trying to cross the Channel. And, of course, the military pilots of today who, despite being surrounded by the latest hi-tech hardware, really have to fly by the seat of their pants when the occasion demands. The occasions, as we shall see, are not only frequent, but have amusing consequences.

Meet the only pilot ever to fly without wings ... and the one who lost his plane and found it again – all in mid-air ...

BY THE SEAT OF HIS PANTS – LITERALLY

In one of the last dog-fights of World War One Canadian pilot Lt. Makepeace zig-zagged all over the sky trying to shake off a pack of German fighters hard on his tail.

In a desperate effort he threw the aircraft into a steep dive that caught his co-pilot Capt. J. Hedley completely unawares. The unfortunate aviator was sucked from his seat and left helpless somewhere in mid-air.

The intrepid Makepeace levelled out, oblivious to the fact that he was now flying solo. As he looked round, Hedley, following close behind in the slipstream, landed with a thump, straddling the tail of the fighter.

UP, UP AND AWAY

In 1785 Frenchman Pierre Blanchard and American Dr John Jeffries prepared to make the first attempt to cross the English Channel by balloon. Watched by a large crowd, they ascended gently and drifted towards France.

The journey was impeded seriously by a huge pair of flapping iron wings hanging on each side of the gondola which, in turn, was navigated with a heavy metal propeller.

Half way across, and within sight of victory, the strange-looking craft began to lose altitude. The sea loomed nearer and, in order to gain height, the aviators dismantled and ditched the metal contraptions.

But even that was not enough. As they glided towards the drink they frantically tore off their heavy topcoats and hats and tossed them overboard. After them they threw their waistcoats and boots.

There was an appropriate decline in their rate of descent by now. But further sacrifice was required. Blanchard and Jeffries took off their trousers and – in a final desperate measure – emptied their bladders over the side of the basket.

It was apparently enough to tip the scales and the pair just cleared the French coast, trouserless but triumphant.

NO WINGS AND A PRAYER

The editors of *Flying* magazine run a column of cautionary tales to help pilots to learn from each other's mistakes. Few, however, are likely to make the error of USAF Commander Franklin Metzner, who took off from a jungle airstrip with the wings of his Skyraider still folded.

It happened in Korea in 1951 when the pilot was ordered to fly to the strip, which was little more than steel mesh laid over a paddyfield, and collect a payload of bombs.

After manhandling them aboard, he checked everything for take-off, except the big red-and-white striped handle marked WING FOLD – it seemed so obvious at the time – and roared down the runway.

Miraculously, he rose to 150 ft, glanced at the wings to check that the flaps were down, and noticed in horror that there weren't any. Metzner cleared a ditch and crash-landed, managing to escape before the aircraft caught fire.

GIVE WAY

Magistrates in the small New South Wales town of Broken Hill heard a case in 1964 against Allan Carmichael, who was charged with driving an aircraft while drunk along a main street.

The court was told that he collided with a police car and used indecent language to the officers trying to arrest him. Mr Carmichael, who was fined £40, plus £4 for his language, said that he had hit a bullock and was driving into town to report the accident.

FRESH TO THE LAST DROP

United States Congresswoman Barbara Boxer demanded to know why the Pentagon had bought hundreds of coffee machines for $7,622 each when the same models were on sale in the shops for $99.50.

It was a reasonable question, and the Pentagon thought about it for a while before offering the following justification: 'The brewer, which contains 2,000 parts, makes ten cups of coffee and is to be installed in the Lockheed C5A. It is a very reliable device and will continue making coffee after loss of cabin pressure following a direct hit.'

DON'T LOOK UP

Peter Tory, the *Daily Mirror*'s flying diary editor, was visiting Dartmoor in 1984 when he noticed an RAF pilot, 30,000 ft up, drawing the unmistakable outline of male genitals across the clear blue sky with his vapour trail.

Air currents in the upper atmosphere soon swelled the size of his artistry to vast proportions. 'By late afternoon,' Tory reported, 'the thing had grown some twelve miles wide by thirty miles long. The pilot found himself, later that day, facing a scalding reprimand.

'What he didn't know was that his commanding officer had been special guest at a ladies' garden party given by a West Country bishop.'

THE ULTIMATE FLYING NIGHTMARE

The horror story beyond a pilot's wildest fantasies happened one night between Omaha and Fort Rucker, Alabama. The man at the controls of the Army TL-19D, 7,000 ft above the mountains of Arkansas, heard a noise from his engine as though someone was trying to smash it with a hammer. The ensuing vibration shook off his headset as he wrestled with the controls.

Suddenly, he told *Flying* magazine, the engine stopped, and he was alone with the eerie noise of the wind for company. After an unsuccessful attempt to restart the engine, the pilot bailed out.

To his relief, his parachute opened safely. As he drifted towards the distant forests he heard a strange whooshing noise – and saw the lights of his own empty aircraft bearing down on him. It passed overhead by a few feet, almost cutting his parachute in two.

Badly shaken, he continued to descend only to see the plane heading towards him again. In desperation he tried to climb his parachute rigging, almost collapsing the chute in the process, as the plane passed beneath his feet.

The astonishing coincidence, he realized, was because the aircraft had one wing fuel tank empty and one full, and was gliding to earth in a great spiral.

As he gave thanks for his deliverance, he saw the lights of the plane approaching a third time. He drew up his legs and swears he saw the lights on the control panel as it left him swaying in its slipstream. To his great relief the TL-19D crashed, allowing him to continue his descent without further interruption.

AIRBORNE ENEMA

A US Army helicopter pilot and co-pilot strayed off course over a fountain which was cascading water hundreds of feet into the air. As they passed over they caught the full force of the blast.

'The pilot was looking one way and the co-pilot the other,' said a spokesman for the Helicopter Foundation International. 'The water blew out the bottom panels of the helicopter and gave the two a real bath.'

BULL'S-EYE

Who says the bow and arrow is no match for the might of an air force? A United Nations helicopter was patrolling a troublespot in Southern Africa when an optimistic local fired a home-made arrow at it.

The arrow hit an oil line, causing the pressure to drop dramatically and the pilot to fight to get his machine to the ground safely.

CHICKEN NUGGETS

In 1984 the Pentagon announced with pride a piece of military hardware which was light years ahead of the Russians.

For the layman, it was a gun which fired dead chickens at aircraft at 700 miles an hour. The 20ft cannon, unveiled at Arnold Air Base, Tennessee, was specifically designed to see how US Air Force jets could withstand the full impact of, um, a dead chicken.

The serious intent behind it was that ten pilots had been killed and £70 million worth of flying hardware lost through bird strikes. As Dermot Purgavie of the *Daily Mail* noted, 'It is alarming to contemplate what would happen if the chicken gun ever fell into the wrong hands.'

One lucky bird-strike survivor was an American helicopter pilot who was flying near Detroit when a bird smashed the machine's Plexiglas windscreen and knocked him senseless. Fortunately, the chopper was on automatic pilot at the time. When he recovered, fifteen minutes later, he was still flying merrily along.

THE FLYING DECKCHAIR

When Larry Walters, thirty-three, decided to build his own flying machine, it was very much a home-made affair. Give or take a few technical specifications, it consisted of forty-two balloons tied to a deckchair.

At 16,000 ft, however, it was enough to make pilots approaching Long Beach, California, radio reports of an unidentified flying object. Walters, fined £2,500 for flying without a licence, told the court in 1982, 'I'm innocent. I never meant to fly so high.'

He explained that he only expected the weather balloons to carry him a few hundred feet. When he found himself soaring skywards at an alarming rate, he descended by shooting them out one by one with an air gun.

STARDUST

About 200 West German Starfighters have crashed
since they were first produced in the late 1950s.
Luftwaffe pilots now have a grim joke:
Q: 'How do you get a Starfighter?'
A: 'Buy a field and wait.'

IS ANYONE OUT THERE?

One Christmas Day an American pilot was on his way
home to New Jersey, flying through a snow storm. He
landed to find the airport deserted – and his cabin door
frozen solid. Despite several efforts to release himself,
he could not budge the door and there was not a soul
in sight.

For two hours, he told *Flying* magazine, he waved a
flashlight at distant cars before giving up in despair. In
a stroke of inspiration he decided to fly to another
airport which was usually guarded by security-men.

He took off in terrible weather conditions to find that
that, too, was closed and empty. Now rather
desperate, he took to the air a third time, asking any
control tower which might still be manned to contact
the police. They arranged to meet him at his original
destination where he was freed, just in time for Boxing
Day celebrations.

SPENDING A PENNY

Small aircraft have all mod cons in a technical sense,
but their compactness of design usually means that

there is no room for the real necessity of flying – a loo. Seasoned pilots always make sure that they spend a penny before take-off, but passengers are not always blessed with the same foresight.

Gerry Marsden, the singer, was on tour in Australia, flying across open country in a small plane, when he mentioned to the pilot that he could not see a loo anywhere on the aircraft.

'There isn't one, mate,' the pilot grinned. 'But not to worry.'

With that he made an immediate landing in the bush, pointed through the window and said, 'Help yourself.'

Lindbergh, who made the first solo non-stop crossing of the Atlantic in thirty-three hours, presumably had a similar problem. When King George V received him at Buckingham Palace in 1927, the same question was on his mind.

'Tell me, Captain Lindbergh,' the King asked confidentially, 'How did you pee?'

The Russians, always a practical people, installed the first airborne lavatory in 1913, aboard a giant transport plane called the *Russky Vitiaz*. Travellers had to use the unpressurized cubicle in Siberian conditions.

NEARER MY GOD TO THEE

Aerospace Medicine reported the case in 1974 of a pilot who confessed to doctors that he was God. The thirty-four-year-old USAF Phantom pilot, an ex-Vietnam war veteran, threw his jet into a series of hair-raising dives to land on imaginary runways. His perspiring navigator finally persuaded him to keep flying as there was not a runway in sight.

CHICKEN POWER

One of the earliest flying pioneers was John Damian, a favourite of King James IV of Scotland, who unsuccessfully took to the air in 1507. He made a wager with friends that he could catch up with an emissary who had set sail for France some days before.

When they asked him, disbelievingly, how he was going to do it, Damian confidently told them, 'I shall fly.' He constructed an enormous pair of wings covered in thousands of feathers from various birds, including chickens.

Three days later he stepped from the battlements of Stirling Castle and dropped to the ground, breaking both his legs. 'I ought to have known,' he fumed as they stretchered him to bed, 'those barn fowls can't fly. I should never have put their feathers on my wings.' He issued orders forthwith that all chickens in his fifedom should have their necks wrung.

At least he tried. One craft which failed to get off the drawing-board was designed in 1835 by Scotsman

Thomas Mackintosh. It took the form of a cigar-shaped balloon with sixteen large birds tethered to the forward section. Mackintosh recommended eagles or geese, trained to the sound of the pilot's voice to pull right at 'gee' and left at 'haw'.

RUNNING REPAIRS

Pilot Scott Gordon was coming in to land at Augustine, Florida, in 1985, when he noticed that one of the wheels on his Piper Turbo-Arrow was stuck. Realizing that he was unable to land, he radioed airport manager Jim Moser for advice.

Moser, a stunt pilot, told him to keep circling while he ran for a high performance car and the help of mechanic Joe Lippo. The plane flew low over the runway with the car travelling immediately beneath it at ninety miles per hour. Joe climbed through the vehicle sun-roof, reached up and yanked down the undercarriage.

When the plane had landed safely he said, 'I grabbed it and pulled as hard as I could – and down it came. I didn't have time to think of the danger. I could never have done it without the talent of the pilot and the driver.'

A MERE TRICKLE

Capt. W. Lawrence Hope, proprietor of an air-taxi in his open bi-plane, published his memoirs in 1930. *Pearson's Weekly* ran them under the heading 'Queer Fares In The Air.'

'In the early hours of a winter's morning,' the captain recalled, 'a woman's voice came over the phone. In her agitation she could hardly speak, but I gathered that she wanted a plane in a quarter of an hour for a long flight. She arrived dressed in black, with the information that she wanted to fly to St Antoine, and demanded to know the fare.

'I discovered by reference to my atlas that there were two places of that name – one in the South of France and one in South America. Taking it for granted that France was to be her destination, I quoted her accordingly.'

When the woman remarked that it was remarkably cheap for Argentina, Hope was taken aback and explained that there was no way in which his flimsy craft could cross the Atlantic.

'Why not?' she demanded. 'We can go across the short way by Newfoundland and then just trickle down the coast.'

'I informed her,' Captain Hope said, 'that the "trickle down the coast" alone was a matter of many thousands of miles. And as for crossing the Atlantic, I was sorry, but that did not come within the province of my aerial taxi.

' "But," she almost shouted, "you don't understand. There has been a death in the family."

' "My dear lady," I replied, "if you take this trip, there will be another death in the family. You should go quietly home, and forget that there are such things as aeroplanes." So away she went, sad and disillusioned.'

TREASURE HUNT

Air crash investigators piece together wrecked aircraft to find out what went wrong – a logical process, as long as they have the pieces. When a United States Air Force F-18 Hornet crashed near Basingstoke in 1980, wreckage was scattered over a wide area. The two-man crew ejected and neither was hurt.

Two vital twelve-inch fragments of turbine wheel could not be accounted for. To encourage locals to search for them, the fighter's manufacturers launched a treasure hunt with a £1,000 prize and £5,000 in donations to charity for the winners.

Chief Inspector Donald Harvey of Basingstoke Police said, 'I have already dug my garden up, but without any luck.'